"*Puppets+Kids+Bible Stories* stirs the imagination, involves the child and connects all to God = Success."

Sister Jeanne Houlihan
Maryknoll, NY

"Anne Neuberger has thoughtfully created a source book for puppet theater that is so tempting I can hardly wait to use it with my religion classes. The suggestions for how to produce puppet plays are especially helpful. The format flexibility, Bible citations, discussion topics, and related prayers will be appreciated by everyone who's interested in creatively teaching their students. Tessie Bundick's well-researched and detailed paper puppets are perfect for coloring and involving imagination. There are even backdrop plants and animals to make the settings more realistic. This book is a 'must have' for every religion teacher's inspiration shelf."

Vicki Palmquist
Children's Literature Specialist

"*Puppets+Kids+Bible Stories* is a treasury every teacher, catechist, or parent needs to help students experience Scripture by using puppets as a teaching tool. Each chapter begins with an appropriate question. The preparation section gives explicit directions for the props and backdrop needed for the story, but also leaves room for creative techniques. The narration is written in 'kid language.' Even the discussion and reflection pieces are visual. The short closing prayer at the end of every chapter is relevant and puts children in touch with the source of their being."

Elizabeth Arend
Director of Faith Formation, Saint John Vianney
South Saint Paul, Minnesota

# Anne E. Neuberger
## illustrated by Tessie Bundick

# Puppets
# +Kids
# +Bible Stories
# =A Creative
# Way to Learn

# TWENTY-THIRD PUBLICATIONS
## A Division of Bayard   MYSTIC, CT 06355

# Dedication

To Peggy Carlson-Robin
who shares my delight in stories and puppets

Twenty-Third Publications
A Division of Bayard
185 Willow Street
P.O. Box 180
Mystic, CT 06355
(860) 536-2611
(800) 321-0411

ISBN:1-58595-132-3
Library of Congress Catalog Card Number: 00-135772
Printed in the U.S.A.

# Contents

# Acknowledgments

The author would like to thank the teachers and students who helped bring these stories to the puppet stage as this book was being written:
Jeanne Bennek and her students, Abraham Jungbauer, Jon Sax, Will Dietzman, Mike Kohler, Elise Kieffer, Annie Bennek, Rosie Murphy, Amanda Daul, Matt Wood, Nick Schwartz, Sara Duxbury, Max Majkowski, Mark Dominik, Katie Hynan, Liam Gallagher, Katie Cox, Ted Kermes, Abby Furlong, Marie Iannazzo, Sarah Redding, Julie Kluge, Brittany Flom, Mike Quinn, Eric Chapin, Jake Lorence, Sarah Fitch, Jessie Zitur, and Bill Struntz, of Saint Mary of the Lake School, and Sue Schmidtbauer and Nancy Guertin and their students, Eric Albrecht, Neil Arcand, Jenna Auckland, Allie Autrey, Matt Bennek, Alex Burris, Dan Cochran, Nick Davern, Beth Gion, Jill Gysberg, Matt Haas, Janelle Hartmann, Megan Hynes, Caitlin Laszewski, Corey Munns, Vince Murphy, Jeff Norton, Tom Opitz, Tricia Rinella, Jessica Rushenberg, Angie Scheller, Teresa Scherping, Joe Schmidt, Ryan Skaar, John Wise, Amy Worobel, Ben Bohnen, Sarah Brogan, Lisa Carr, Natalie Casemore, Lara Conrad, Mary Hamilton, Katrina Heimerl, Jessica Higgins, Charlie Igo, Matt Johnson, Brandon Kohler, Stephanie Majkowski, Craig Malek, Melissa Morency, Kristina O'Hern, Kristin Paul, Christine Price, Thomas Ramaekers, Joe Rauchbauer, Joseph Reil, Bill Sand, Jessica Shaw, Andrew Thompson, Steve Turnbull, and Sarah A. Zweber, of Holy Family Middle School.

# Puppets + Kids + Bible Stories
# = A Creative Way to Learn

# Introduction

## The Need for Story and Imagination

Stories have been around since the beginning of humankind. In past generations, children were told Bible stories, folk tales, and anecdotes about their ancestors. Stories help educate our emotional side, which may be why Jesus taught in parables. By appealing to our feelings stories stay with us longer and affect us more profoundly than teachings that are purely rational. Over the centuries, stories have not lost their power to teach, heal, encourage, challenge, advise, and entertain.

Stories also help develop the imagination, which brings delight and pleasure in childhood but plays an important role in adulthood, too. The imagination is the ability to think in images. Without it, we cannot develop a sense of compassion because we cannot imagine our neighbor's plight. The lack of imagination may even hinder the ability to love because we cannot see another's full potential. Without imagination we will take no initiative, for we cannot see the possibilities for growth and development. And we need imagination to think in analogies, which is the only way we can think of God.

The need for stories has not changed. However today's children hear fewer stories, and these are often conveyed through movies and television shows. Certain shows are excellent, but many do not contain the richness of traditional storytelling, nor do they often enhance the imagination. In any case, these stories are a passive experience.

### Puppets of Old

Puppetry offers a good alternative to this passivity. Puppets engage the audience and challenge the puppeteers. Their enchantment reaches out to all people. Puppets have touched the hearts of royalty, peasants, sages, and fools. They have brought their magic to street corners, palaces, theaters, churches, splendid cities, and simple villages across the world. Originally, puppets were probably used for religious reasons, not for entertainment. At one time in India, it was believed that puppets were holy—little divine creatures.

Archaeologists have discovered marionettes in Egyptian tombs, and in the ruins of Greece and Rome. The very first marionettes, which were terra cotta dolls with moveable arms and legs, may have been made in China. Centuries later, when the explorer Cortez arrived in what is now Mexico, he brought a puppeteer along, but the indigenous people there were already using puppets in religious ceremonies. Puppets have played a part in storytelling and theater in countries as diverse as Java, Spain, Burma, France, Turkey, Japan, Persia, Russia, India, Germany, and England.

### Puppets and the Church

Puppets have entertained, passed down legends, and poked fun at political figures for centuries in the secular world, but they also have a long history in the Christian Church. Before reading and writing became common skills, Scripture stories were frequently acted out, and puppet shows were often performed in churches for those who could not read. In the ninth century, there were crosses bearing figures of Christ that could move, and whole scenes from the Passion were acted out with puppets. The story of the Nativity was also done with puppetry. Puppet shows in Sicily told of conflicts between Christians and Muslims. For more than three hundred years, puppeteers in Poland have created religious shows. Even the word "marionette" has a religious connection: it was inspired by small statues of the Virgin Mary. During the Middle Ages, many people had extremely beautiful statues of Mary in their homes. They would compare the statues to puppets they saw, thus the word marionette, or "Little Mary," came into being.

## Using This Book

With this book, you can carry on the tradition of teaching Scripture and other religious stories through puppetry. Here is a selection of puppet plays based on stories from the Old and New Testaments. They can be used in religious education programs, Catholic schools, parish retreats, summer Bible school programs, home settings, after-school daycares, and even birthday parties.

The shows are designed with the skills of kindergartners through fifth graders in mind. However, they are not at all limited to these age groups. For example, middle schoolers have enjoyed performing them for preschool and elementary children. You will find that the scripts vary in skill levels. This is so younger children can perform some without frustration, and older children can enjoy the challenge of those that are more involved.

Whatever age the puppeteers are, they immerse themselves in these tales. They will touch on aspects of history and geography through the clothing of the puppets and by drawing the backdrops. The more contact children have with a story, the more it becomes their own. Whether they create puppets and scenery, or perform as puppeteers or narrators, children invest themselves in the characters and stories. They will always remember them. Each story and chapter also includes a short prayer that you can use before or after the story. In addition, there are questions to accompany each story. These can be used as an introduction and follow up, to help the children glean more from the story and apply the lesson to their lives. See end of Additional Ideas section for other ways to use the stories and drawings.

The pages of this book are perforated to make it easier to copy/enlarge puppet figures, and even to copy pages of the script for your class.

# Creating Basic Puppet Shows

These puppet shows are devised for very simple performances with stick puppets and poster board backdrops. Each play is divided into scenes; the information about which puppets and what kind of backdrop are needed precede the script for that scene. You, the stage director, need to decide how many puppeteers are needed, since older children can handle more puppets than younger ones, some stages are larger than others, and so on.

## The Puppets

Along with each script are illustrations of the story characters done in line drawings. These will make excellent stick puppets, the simplest puppets of all. Copy the puppets onto stiff paper. Have children color them with markers. After cutting them out, attach a stick with adhesive tape onto the back of each puppet. Chopsticks work especially well because they are slender and long. A wide puppet may need two sticks. If the audience is to be fairly large, enlarge the puppets so everyone will be able to see them. Use paint stir sticks as the "backbone" and handle for these larger puppets so they do not flop over in the middle of a scene.

## The Puppeteers

While these are simple performances that you can do during religion class, you will need to practice a few times before you invite an audience in. Help children understand that they must have the puppets face the audience at all times. After they have run through the story the first time, have someone else act the puppets while your puppeteers watch. They will better understand the audience's perspective then. Also, it is inevitable with young puppeteers that they may be seen by the audience some or all of the time. That's fine. These shows are designed so children can have creative fun. The results may not be very professional, but the stories will be shared, and the audience will delight in the spontaneity and creativity of the puppet troupe!

## The Narrator

All the puppet scripts are written with only a narrator having a speaking part. This keeps the plays particularly easy to perform. Puppeteers need not learn lines or project their voices, so they can concentrate on having the puppets in the right place at the right time. An adult can narrate if none of the children are fluent enough at reading to do so. The narrator should stand near the puppet stage and read from the script.

The role of the narrator is an important one. It is imperative that this person be an expressive reader. The narrator gives cues to the puppeteers. All of their movements depend on the narrator's reading. The narrator sets the tone at different parts of the play, making it dramatic, funny, exciting, or quiet. For example, when reading that Noah and his family are working very hard to build the ark, the narrator can sound and appear to become exhausted during that paragraph. In some plays, the narrator can invite audience participation and gently end it when necessary. If the audience includes particularly young children, the narrator may choose to define certain words, or further explain a circumstance that will help them better understand the story.

In addition, the narrator is the wise person, the sage who passes on knowledge: for example, that we are all descendants of Abraham and Sarah; or who applies the lesson to us, as in the Jonah story. It would bring dignity and delight to the plays if the narrator dressed as the wise storyteller, perhaps in clothing from biblical times.

## Stages

While some children are coloring the puppets, others can be creating a stage. Keep in mind these factors:

the height of your puppeteers, where the audience will sit, and the width of the surface the puppets stand behind. Too wide a surface, such as a table or desk top, makes it difficult for the audience to see the puppets' movements.

Perhaps you already have access to a puppet theater. If not, here are some simple suggestions for creating one:

• Place a square or rectangular folding table on its side, the table top facing the audience. The two bottom legs should be extended to hold the table up, but the top ones can remain closed to give the puppeteers more room. Hang a sheet or blanket over the table top. Puppeteers sit between the table legs. This will work well for stories that do not need props sitting on a wider surface (such as the ark would need in the Noah story).

• A long bench or a board laid across two chairs, with a sheet or blanket covering the flat surface, can easily become a theater that even the youngest children can "construct."

• Large, cardboard boxes can be decorated with paint. A box that is as large as a table top but only a foot wide makes a good stage. Small puppeteers can even stand behind it, and it offers enough of a ledge to fasten props.

• Make the more traditional box theater from a packing box for a refrigerator. Stand it upright, cut a "window" in it large enough to accommodate your puppet show, but leave the resulting "shutters" attached to it. Keep the shutters closed until the show starts.

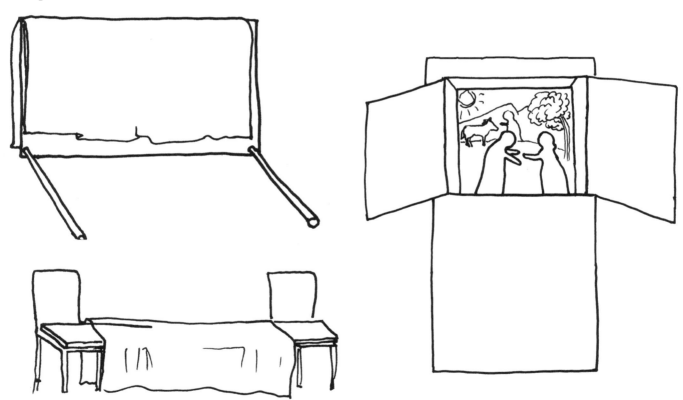

## Backdrops

Each script has suggestions for backdrops which help set the scene. Poster board will work well. For the folding table or bench type stages, place a flip chart stand behind the puppeteers and attach the backdrop. If there is more than one scene, attach every backdrop and just remove them as each scene is completed. For a traditional theater found in libraries or schools, or for the refrigerator box theater, the backdrop can be taped to the back. Another method would be to fasten the backdrop to a dowel with long strips of strong tape. Then lay the dowel across the top of the theater.

Some of the suggestions for creating the backdrop will require a small amount of research on the part of the artists. Through picture Bibles or encyclopedias, they can see how Bethlehem looked in the days of Jesus, or what type of tent Abraham and Sarah lived in, etc. Other backdrops, such as the fiery furnace of the Shadrach story, invite imagination and the use of lots of color!

## Additional Ideas

Puppet shows can be as simple or as elaborate as you want to make them. Here are some suggestions for a variety of methods that can be used with these scripts.

• Have someone play music (piano, violin, autoharp, guitar, etc.) before the show, or between shows.

• Make hand puppets (see pattern). Making these puppets invites more involved creativity than stick puppets, and hand puppets allow for more activity on the stage. Some sewing is involved as the fronts and backs must be stitched together by hand or machine. Use felt, old blue jeans, or any other stiff fabric to create the body, and yarn for hair. (You can also make sock puppets out of old socks.) Use felt scraps to create faces, hands, and clothing by gluing them to the body. Sequins, buttons, and fabric paint can add interest and details.

• Tiny dolls can be used as puppets. Create these by purchasing wooden forms from a craft store. These are about 2 to 3 inches high, and have a head and peg-like body. Make them into the appropriate characters with felt, glue, pipe cleaners, acrylic paint, etc. The puppet stage would simply be a low table, decorated to reflect the story, with trees, houses, etc. made of painted shoeboxes, clay, twigs, pine cones, etc. The puppeteer is completely visible, sitting behind the table and walking the puppet dolls through the story. The puppeteer can tell the story, or a narrator can read the script. This type of show works well with very young children. The stage should be covered with a light, colorful cloth before the puppet show. The show begins when the cloth is lifted.

• The narrator's role could be performed by a puppet. This would add a greater sense of the magic of puppetry and would especially engage the youngest audience members. However, a stick puppet would not suffice for the narrator, for this puppet must have greater movement. Make a more elaborate sock puppet or create a hand puppet with a three-dimensional head. Make the body similar to the hand puppet pattern, except make a neck instead of a head. Create the head by applying papier mâché to a small, inflated balloon. The head must be correctly proportioned to the body. The whole puppet must be scaled to fit the puppeteer's hand, so decide if a child or an adult will move this puppet. Leave an opening in the papier mâché, about a one and one half inch wide circle around the mouth of the balloon. Once the papier mâché is thoroughly dry, prick the balloon to deflate it, then remove it. Make a neck out of cardboard or stiff paper, creating a small tube, large enough for two fingers to slip into. Insert the neck about one inch into the opening in the head. Do another layer of papier mâché, including the neck this time. When this layer is dry, paint the head with acrylic paints, add hair (use yarn or cotton balls or small doll wigs sold in craft stores). Attach the head to the body by sliding the neck on the head into the neck on the body. Fasten with glue. In making this puppet, think about its character before you paint the face or make the clothes on the body. A wise old woman or man might be appropriate, or a wild prophet like Elijah or John the Baptist would be fun, too. When using a puppet narrator, you may want to provide a separate stage so the puppeteer is not seen.

• The puppet figures in this book can also be used as paper dolls.

• Any of these puppets can be used for flannel board stories if they are backed with sandpaper or felt.

# God's Masterpiece

## A Story of Creation

Based on Genesis 1, 2:1–4

### Questions to discuss before the story

Name ten things—not made by people—that we need to live on this earth. Now choose three of those ten. What would life be like without these gifts from God?

Here's the story about God's creation.

### Preparation: Scene 1

*Puppets.* The gazelles, monkeys, lizards, cheetahs, sloths, and people.

*Props.* Back these cut-outs with strips of light sandpaper so they can adhere to a flannelboard: a water border that spans the flannelboard, clouds, a lake with different kinds of fish, trees, flowers, grasses, sun, moon and stars, and birds.

*Backdrop.* Because this story does not include stick puppets until the very end, it requires a different type of backdrop from the other stories. A flannelboard (3'x3') would work well. Dividing it in half vertically, cover one side with light blue felt or flannel, and the other side with very dark blue. These will represent day and night. The water border should be placed horizontally along the bottom of the flannelboard. The flannelboard could be placed on a large easel, but you will need a stage in front of it (such as a folding table) since most of the puppeteers will need to stand or kneel behind something.

*Tips for this scene.* One puppeteer will need to stand and place the props onto the board. Since this person will be seen, he or she may want to wear something very dark so as to attract as little attention as possible.

*Enter the narrator who stands in front of the stage.*

| | |
|---|---|
| Narrator | Before there was anything at all, before there was time or place, there was God. There were no winters or summers, trees or gardens, cars or computers. There were no people, no songs, no sound. There was only God, the Creator. God's spirit hovered over the deep, dark waters. Then God said, "Let there be light!" *The narrator moves to the side of the stage and a puppeteer places the flannelboard onto the easel. The narrator gestures towards the flannelboard.* |
| Narrator | And there was light! God called the light "day" and the dark "night." And that was the first day!  *Narrator encourages the audience to repeat "That was the first day!"* |
| Narrator | Then God said, "Let there be a great space above the waters." That was the second day! *In the light blue section of the flannelboard, a puppeteer places clouds in the sky.* |
| Narrator | And the Creator called this the sky. That was the second day. |
| Audience | That was the second day. |
| Narrator | Then God said, "Let dry land appear. Let the earth bring forth growing things." *A puppeteer removes the water border and adds the objects as they are named.* |
| Narrator | And great trees, beautiful flowers, and waving grasses began to grow. And that was the third day! |
| Audience | And that was the third day. |
| Narrator | The next day, God said, "Let there be light in the heavens!" *A puppeteer adds the objects onto the appropriate places on the flannelboard as they are named.* |

| Narrator | And there came to be a warming sun for the daytime. And a moon and stars to gently light the night. And that was the fourth day! |
|---|---|
| Audience | And that was the fourth day. |
| Narrator | "Now," God said, "Let the waters teem with fish of all sizes and colors!" *A puppeteer adds the lake with the fish.* |
| Narrator | "And let the sky be filled with the flight and song of birds!" And that was the fifth day! *A puppeteer places the birds in the skies.* |
| Audience | And that was the fifth day. |
| Narrator | Then God made other animals. *These stick puppets can enter as the narrator names them and move about in front of the flannelboard until the end of the scene.* |
| Narrator | There came galloping gazelles, mischievous monkeys, leaping lizards, chasing cheetahs, slow sloths and many, many more kinds of creatures. It was all so wonderful. But God was not quite finished. God said, "Let us make human beings in our image." And so God created people, man and woman. *Enter human puppets.* |
| Narrator | They came to life because of God's love. They were beautiful because they were made in God's image. And God looked around *(narrator gestures first towards stage and then toward the audience, to include them in the Creation)*. God saw that it was good. It was all very good. That was the sixth day! |
| Audience | That was the sixth day. |
| Narrator | And on the seventh day, God rested. |

## For discussion and reflection

How can you help take care of the gifts of God's creation?

## Closing prayer

All creation is a sign of God's great love. Let us say a thanksgiving prayer for what God has given us.

Thank you, God our Creator, for_____.

(Some suggestions: clouds, mountains, eagles, oak trees, elephants, rain, apples.)

*All:* Amen.

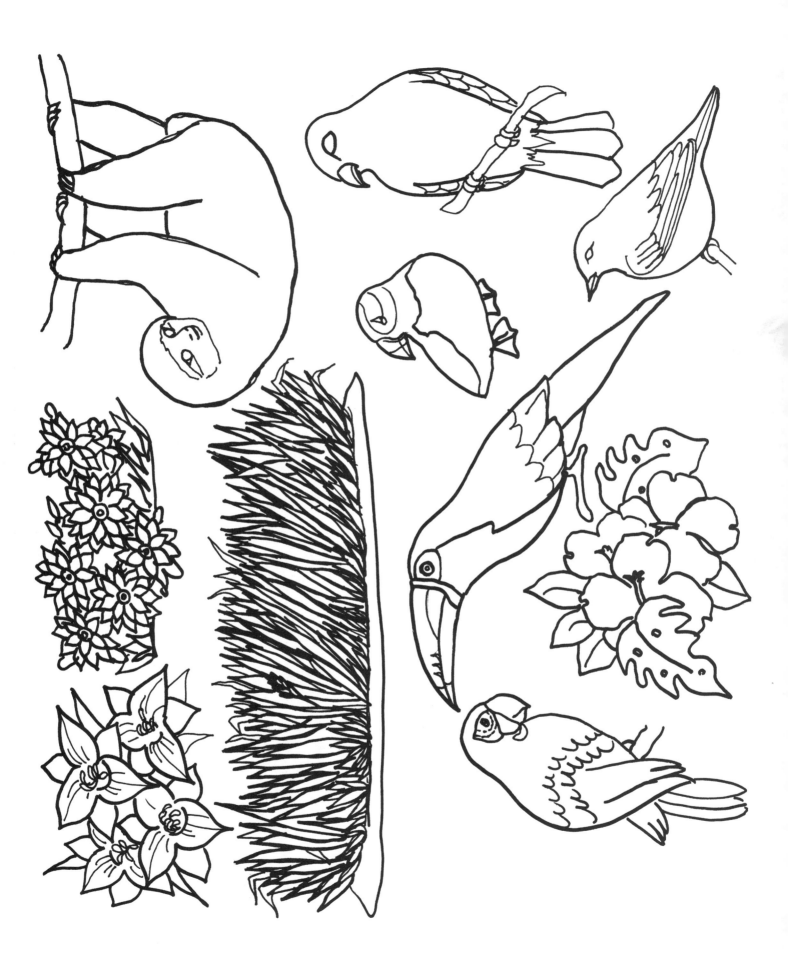

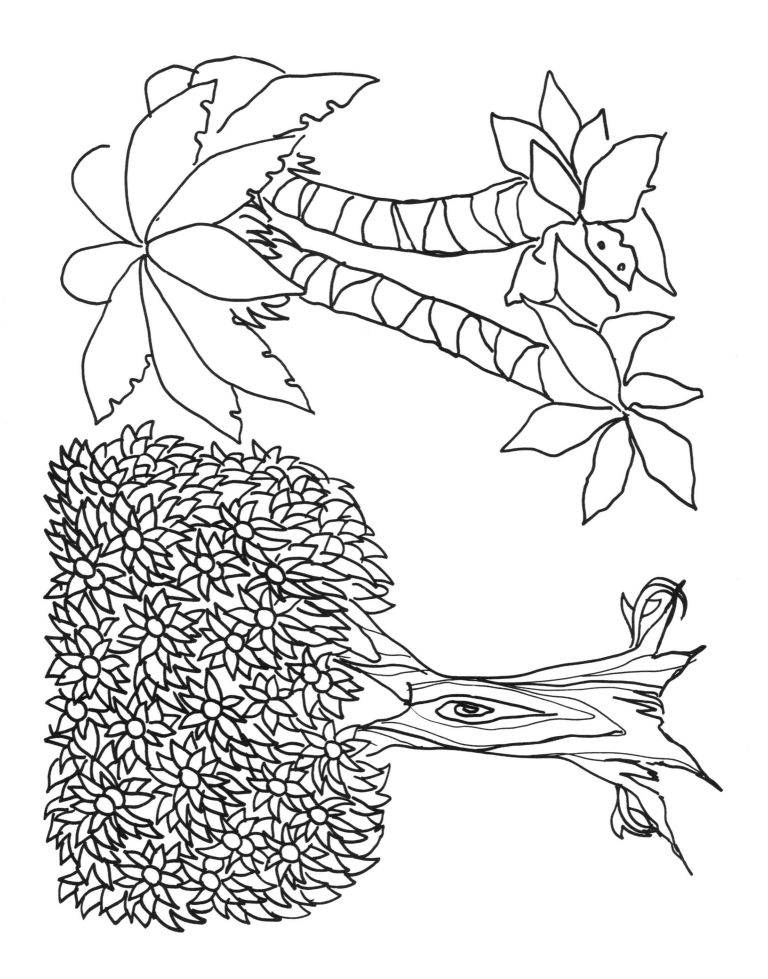

# A Big Boat for Big Rain

## A Story of Noah's Family

Based on Genesis 6, 7, 8, and 9

### Questions to discuss before the story

Have you ever been soaked in a rain storm? Have you ever been in or seen a flood? Watch to learn who survives the flood in this story.

### Preparation: Scene 1

*Puppets.* Noah and his wife, their son Shem and his wife, their son Japheth and his wife, and their son Ham and his wife, a group of observers, and the giraffes, hippos, birds, snakes, sheep, and kangaroo puppets (the single dove puppet can remain below).

*Props.* The ark pattern is smaller than needed. Enlarge it to the correct size for your puppets. Brown poster board would work well. Attach the ark to the end of an inverted shoe box that is slightly smaller than the ark. The ark should face the audience. Cut small slits in the upturned bottom of the box so the sticks on the animal puppets can be slid into the slits. They will then be held upright without the aid of a puppeteer. The ramp can be attached to the side of the ark for animals to "walk up." Attach it to the side so the animal puppets can go up face first. Take it off when all are inside.

*Backdrop.* Blue poster board with a bright sun.

*Tips for this scene.* Have the audience make hammering and sawing motions at the appropriate time.

*The narrator stands to the side of the stage.*

| | |
|---|---|
| Narrator | When the world was still young, there lived a family that loved God. *Enter Noah and wife puppet, and all three sons and wives puppets.* |
| Narrator | Noah's family tried to live as God asked. Now this was not easy. All the other people had chosen to be very bad. *Enter the observers puppet.* |
| Narrator | God looked sadly at this world of evil. God decided to start over. He would send a great flood to cover the earth. Only the people who loved God would survive. They would have to build a huge boat, called an ark. God told Noah's family to do this. *Bring up the ark and place it in the center of the stage.* |
| Narrator | They hammered and sawed and measured. They smeared tar on all the cracks. That way, water could not leak in. *All the Noah puppets are busy, scurrying about the ark. The observers puppet stands to the side.* |
| Narrator | While they worked, the other people made fun of them. "There's not a cloud in the sky!" they jeered. "You are crazy!" Still, Noah's family kept on working. Finally the ark was finished. *Exit observers puppet.* |
| Narrator | And then the real work began! God told them to gather all the animals of the earth and skies. God said to bring two of each animal onto the ark. *Attach the ramp to the ark with a piece of tape. All the puppets that are Noah's family go below and each brings back animal pairs and brings them into the ark, placing the animals into the slits in the box. Puppeteers can make animal sounds.* |
| Narrator | Finally all the animals and Noah's family were in the ark. Then it began to rain. *Pull ramp into the ark. All remain on stage. Change backdrop for Scene 2.* |

## Preparation: Scene 2

*Puppets.* The Noah puppets and the animals puppets (except the dove).

*Props.* Use a rain stick to add auditory interest to this scene. To make a rain stick: Take a long cardboard tube from gift wrap and push many straight pins through the sides until the tops of the pins are flush with the tube. Then fill one-third of the tube with dried beans and rice. Cover the ends of the tube with plastic wrap and secure with rubber bands. The rain stick can be decorated with markers or paint. To "play," slowly move the stick so the contents slip down, imitating the sound of rain.

*Backdrop.* Gray poster board with clouds drawn on it.

*Tips for this scene.* As there is not much action here, engage the audience with sounds as indicated.

| | |
|---|---|
| Narrator | *(begins using the rain stick)* It rained, and rained, and rained, and rained. *Encourage audience to repeat:* It rained, and rained, and rained, and rained. |
| Narrator | Then it rained and rained and rained some more! |
| Audience | (repeat) Then it rained and rained and rained some more! |
| Narrator | *(Continue with rain stick.)* Sometimes it thundered. *Have audience make clapping sounds. A puppeteer can gently move the ark back and forth as if it were floating.* |
| Narrator | It rained for forty long days and forty long nights. Noah and his family and all the animals waited. They wanted so much to see dry land and sunshine. *Scene ends with people, animals, and ark remaining on the stage. Change backdrop to Scene 3.* |

## Preparation: Scene 3

*Puppets.* All the puppets from Scene 2 and the dove puppet.

*Props.* Have the rainbow ready with tape on the back of it. One puppeteer can reach up and place the rainbow on the backdrop at the appropriate time. The ramp will need to be put back on.

*Backdrop.* Blue sky with sun shining. Plan for where you will place the rainbow.

| | |
|---|---|
| Narrator | Finally, the rain stopped. Slowly the water went down. Noah let a dove go. *Dove puppet flies beyond ark and returns.* |
| Narrator | The dove came back with a branch with green leaves. This meant plants and trees were growing again! Noah and his family cheered! *Puppets dance a bit.* |
| Narrator | It was time to let the animals out. *Put the ramp back out on the opposite side so the animal puppets run down or fly off, including the dove. The animals all exit the stage as they leave the ark.* |
| Narrator | Oh, what a noise! *Audience can make thundering sounds by stamping feet.* |
| Narrator | And then, it was quiet and peaceful. Noah's family got off the ark. *The people puppets stand next to the ark and thank God.* |
| Narrator | And God said, "I will make a promise, a covenant, with you, my people. I will never again send another flood like this. I will place a rainbow in the sky. *Place rainbow onto the poster board.* |
| Narrator | "The rainbow will be a sign to everyone of this promise." |
| Narrator | (to audience) Now every time you see a rainbow, you can remember God's great love for us. *Exit all puppets.* |

**For discussion and reflection**

Why did God send the flood? What did God promise Noah after the flood? What does God promise us if we live as God wants us to live?

**Closing prayer**

Dear God, your rainbow reminds us of your love and care for us, which will never end. Thank you, God; we love you.

*All:* Amen.

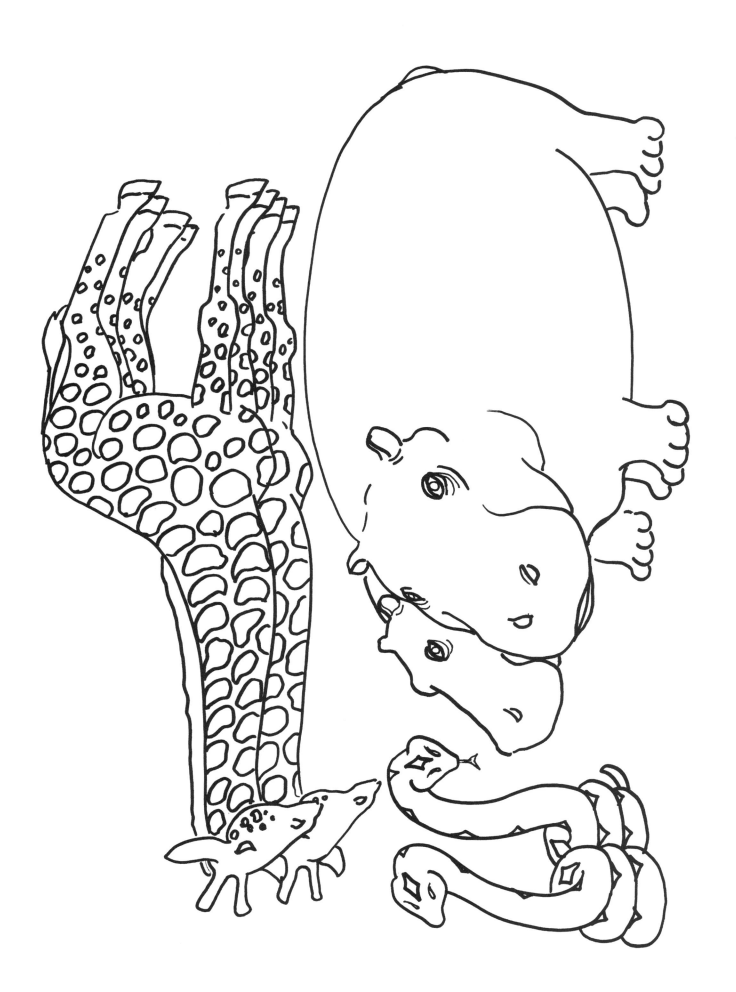

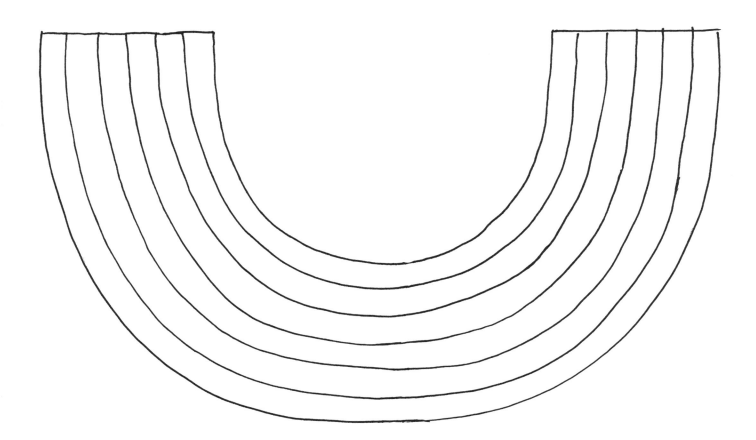

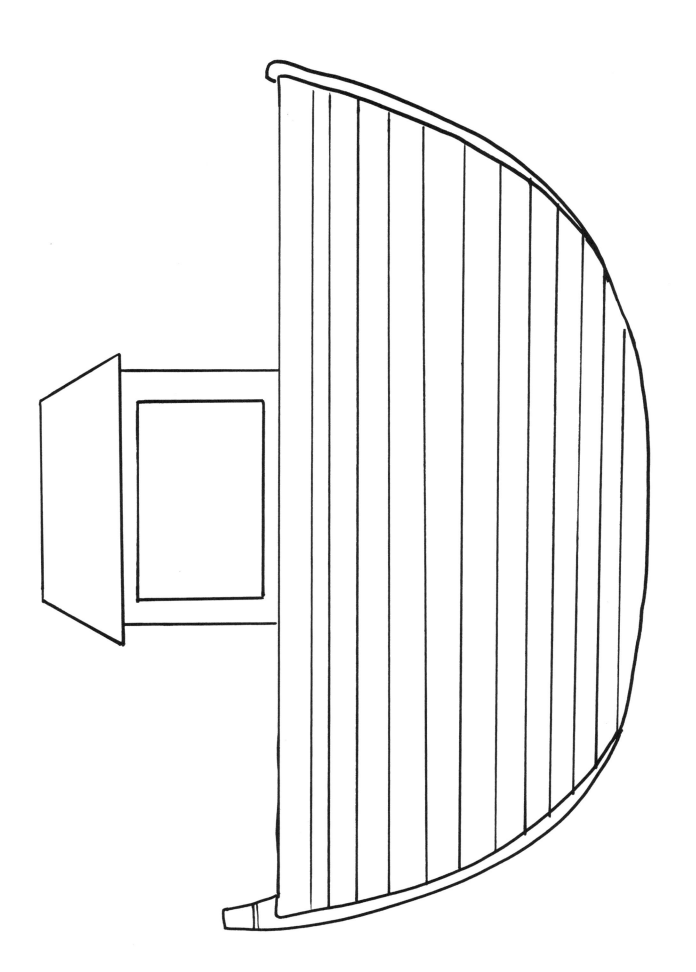

# As Many as The Stars

## A Story of Sarah and Abraham's Family

Based on Genesis 15 and 18

### Questions to discuss before the story

Have your parents or grandparents ever told you stories about when they were children? Where they lived, what they hoped for?

### Preparation: Scene 1

*Puppet.* Abraham looking up to heaven.

*Backdrop.* Dark blue poster board covered with many adhesive stars.

*Tips for this scene.* There should be a feeling of quiet and reverence on Abraham's part. God's voice should portray love and authority, Abraham's should be respectful but puzzled. If the audience is made up of pre-school through first graders, they could be "stars." When God tells Abraham that his descendants will be as numerous as the stars, children can make their hands twinkle like stars. Have them hold their hands above their heads, closed into a fist, then open them, again and again. Another method would be to draw stars on the palms of their hands in washable markers. This will help them understand that they are also Abraham's descendants.

*The narrator stands to the side of the stage.*

| | |
|---|---|
| Narrator | Long, long ago, most people did not know there is only one God. They believed that there were many gods. They made up stories about these gods. But there was one couple who believed in one true God. Their names were Abraham and Sarah. God had spoken to them. God gave them directions about where to live. They did what God asked of them. *Enter Abraham.* |
| Narrator | One starry night, Abraham stood outside of their tent. Again he listened for God. And God spoke. "You are a faithful servant, Abraham. I will bless you and your children. I will bless your children's children's children." Abraham answered, "God, Sarah and I pray. We try to do as you ask. But we have no children for you to bless." God said, "Look up, Abraham. See the stars? Count them." Abraham gazed at the stars. There were too many to count. *Children can make stars with their hands.* |
| Narrator | God went on, "You will have as many descendants as the stars. Your children's children's children will be too many to count." *Abraham gazes up for a moment of silence, then exits.* |

### Preparation: Scene 2

*Puppets.* Sarah, Abraham with hands reaching out, three strangers, baby Isaac.

*Props.* A drawing of a plate of food.

*Backdrop.* Light blue poster board. Drawn on the left side is a tent, with the inside fully visible. An illustrated children's Bible may give artists a good idea of the type of tent needed. It must be large enough for the Sarah puppet to stand in. Bedding and cooking utensils can be seen in it. There should be a table for Sarah to knead bread, with bread dough drawn on it. Outside of the tent, draw a large tree that the puppets can stand under.

*Tips for this scene.* Abraham is greatly excited. The Abraham puppeteer should have him be in a flutter of activity. The plate of food and the baby Isaac puppets can be attached to the other puppets with two-sided tape.

*Enter Sarah so she is standing in the tent. Enter Abraham just outside of the tent.*

Narrator    One hot day, Sarah was resting in their tent. Abraham was resting just outside of the tent. Suddenly he saw three people coming. "Sarah!" Abraham called excitedly. "We have company!" *Enter three strangers from the right.*

Narrator    "Welcome, welcome!" Abraham said. "Please stop and rest here! Rest under the tree. It is so hot! We will get you everything you need!" Abraham began running around. He asked Sarah to make bread. *Abraham goes into the tent briefly, exits on left side. Attach food puppet to Abraham. He enters and joins three strangers.*

Narrator    "Here, please eat, enjoy!" Abraham said happily. "Where is your wife Sarah?" one guest asked. "She is making bread in our tent," Abraham said. "Do you like rolls? She is making rolls!" Inside the tent, Sarah was listening. *Edge Sarah over to wall of tent to listen.*

Narrator    The guest said, "I will come back next year. Then Sarah will have a baby boy." When Sarah heard this, she laughed to herself. She was going to have a baby? Sarah had always longed for a child. But now she was too old to have a baby! Then the stranger said, "Why did Sarah laugh? God can do everything. God can give Sarah a baby." Now Sarah was afraid. Who was this stranger? "I did not laugh," she called out. But the stranger answered, "Oh, yes you did!" Then the three strangers left. *Exit three strangers to the right. Then exit Abraham and Sarah to the left.*

Narrator    And a wonderful thing happened. A year later Sarah and Abraham did have a baby! *Enter Abraham and Sarah with Isaac puppet attached to Sarah. They stand outside of the tent.*

Narrator    They named the baby "Isaac," which means "laughter." Now Abraham and Sarah's descendants live all over the world. And some of them are sitting here today! *Gesture to include the audience.*

## For discussion and reflection

What did God promise Abraham and Sarah? Why did Abraham and Sarah believe God? Why should we trust in God?

## Closing prayer

Dear God, you told Abraham, "I will bless you and your children and your children's children's children." May we live together peacefully as your children.

*All:* Amen.

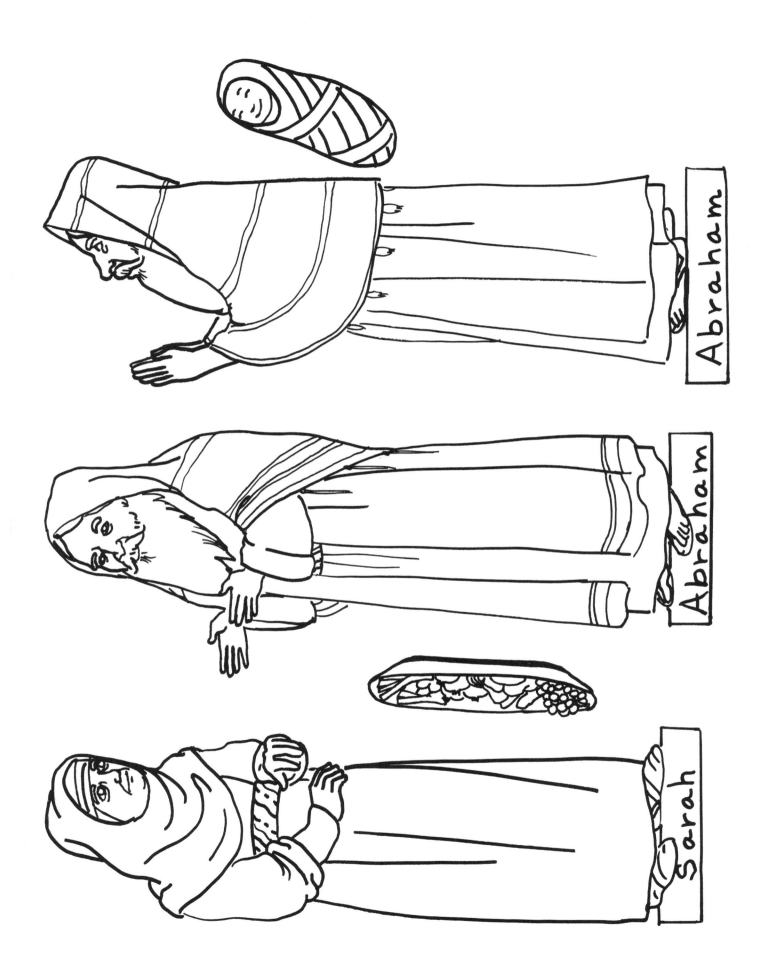

Three Strangers

# The Baby in a Basket

## A Story of Moses and Miriam

Based on Exodus 1 and 2

### Questions to discuss before the story

What kinds of things does your mother do that show she loves you?

### Preparation: Scene 1

*Puppets.* Mother, Miriam looking over her shoulder, basket with baby Moses.

*Backdrop.* Light brown poster board, with drawings of a simple home.

| | |
|---|---|
| Narrator | *(standing in front of the empty stage)* Long ago in Egypt, the pharaoh, or king, was worried. In this land lived his own people, the Egyptians, and also the Hebrews. The more the number of Hebrews grew, the more nervous the pharaoh became. What if they became more powerful than the Egyptians? They might take over! So, the pharaoh came up with an evil plan. He said that all Hebrew baby boys must be killed! Our story is about one such baby whose clever mother and brave sister save him. When the baby grew up, he would save the rest of the Hebrew people. *The narrator moves to stand beside the stage. Enter mother with the basket with baby Moses in it. She works on fixing the basket.* |
| Narrator | In a small house of a poor Hebrew family, a woman was fixing a basket. *Enter Miriam from left.* |
| Narrator | Her daughter Miriam came in. "What are you doing, Mother?" asked Miriam. "We can't keep your baby brother here during the day any longer," said the mother. "Soon the Egyptians will find him. Our only chance of saving him is to hide him in this basket. We will float it in the water. We'll hide the basket in the reeds by the river bank. Come with me, Miriam. Your brother may need you."*Attach the basket to the mother with tape. Exit Miriam and mother with the basket.* |

### Preparation: Scene 2

*Puppets.* Mother, Miriam looking forward, basket with baby Moses, pharaoh's daughter, servant woman.

*Prop.* Long strip of reeds and water. This can be copied more than once, depending on the length of the stage.

*Backdrop.* Poster board drawn to look like the opposite river bank.

*Tips for this scene.* Attach the strip of reeds and water to the front of the stage with pins or tape so it appears that the action takes place in the water. A puppeteer will need to reach up to attach the baby basket at different times.

*Enter mother carrying basket, and Miriam from the left, behind the water.*

| | |
|---|---|
| Narrator | Miriam and her mother reached the river bank. Miriam looked around. She saw no one was there. Then her mother kissed the baby and put him and the basket into the reeds. *Attach the basket to the water.* |
| Narrator | Miriam found a hiding place. *Miriam moves further down the stage and sinks down a little, but audience should still see her.* |
| Narrator | "Watch over him, my daughter," her mother said softly. She hurried away so no one would |

| | see her. *Exit mother.* |
|---|---|
| Narrator | For a while, all was quiet. The baby slept. No one came to the river. Then Miriam heard voices. Someone was coming. *Enter pharaoh's daughter and servant woman from the right, behind the water.* |
| Narrator | Miriam could see who it was, and she gasped. The pharaoh's own daughter was coming to the river to bathe! Miriam kept very still and hoped her little brother would not cry. But soon, the pharaoh's daughter saw the basket. And the baby began to cry! *Pharaoh's daughter and servant woman come over to the basket.* |
| Narrator | Miriam watched anxiously. What would the pharaoh's daughter do? Miriam heard her say, "Oh, look. It is one of the Hebrews' children. Poor baby!" When Miriam heard that, she ran to the pharaoh's daughter. *Miriam jumps up from hiding place, comes over to the other puppets.* |
| Narrator | Bravely, Miriam asked, "Shall I find a Hebrew woman to take care of the baby for you?" "Oh, yes!" said the pharaoh's daughter, as she admired the baby. *Exit Miriam who reenters with her mother.* |
| Narrator | The pharaoh's daughter said, "Take this baby to your home and care for him. Bring him to me when he is older. Then I will adopt him." *Exit pharaoh's daughter and servant woman.* |
| Narrator | Miriam and her mother looked at the baby. "He is ours for a while longer, Miriam," said her mother. "Perhaps someday he will do great things for our people." *Attach the basket with baby Moses to the mother. Exit Miriam, mother, and baby.* |

## For discussion and reflection

Why did Moses' mother let the pharaoh's daughter take her baby? Do you think this was hard for her to do? How did saving her baby also help her people?

## Closing prayer

Lord, you love all of your people, no matter who they are. Help us to love that way, too. Help us show others your loving ways.

*All:* Amen.

# Shepherd, Singer, and Warrior

## A Story of David

Based on 1 Samuel 16 and 17

**Questions to discuss before the story**

Do you have any heroes? What do you admire about them?

**Preparation: Scene 1**

*Puppets.* David with arm raised (slingshot), David with hands reaching out (harp), lion, sheep.

*Props.* Harp, slingshot.

*Backdrop.* Scene 1: Dark poster board with stars on it.

*Tips for this scene.* Place a piece of two-sided tape on the harp and slingshot so these can easily be attached to David.

*Note: Five different "David figures" are provided for this story: two for scene 1; one for scene 2; and two for scene 3. You may choose to use only a few of them.*

*Narrator stands to the side of the stage. Enter David with slingshot and sheep.*

| | |
|---|---|
| Narrator | One starry night, a boy named David was watching over his father's sheep in the fields. Everything was quiet. David sensed danger was lurking. Suddenly, a lion sprang out at the sheep! *Enter lion.* |
| Narrator | David had his slingshot. Zing! He shot a stone at the lion with such force that the lion fell down dead. *Lion falls down.* |
| Narrator | The sheep were badly frightened. David put down his slingshot. *David with slingshot exits David with harp enters.* |
| Narrator | David played his harp and sang in a beautiful voice, "The Lord is my shepherd. I shall not want...." And the stars shone down on him. *Exit David and sheep.* |

**Preparation: Scene 2**

*Puppets.* David with hands folded, Samuel, Jesse.

*Backdrop.* Light brown poster board with a street in Bethlehem on the left side leading to Jesse's house. The inside of the home should be drawn so the three puppets can stand in front of it and appear to all fit in easily.

*Enter Samuel.*

| | |
|---|---|
| Narrator | God told the prophet Samuel to go to Bethlehem. Samuel went to the home of a man named Jesse. *Enter Jesse.* |
| Narrator | Jesse had several sons. God had chosen one of them to be the next king. God told Samuel to ask for the youngest son, David, the shepherd. *Enter David.* |
| Narrator | Samuel anointed David with oil. This meant that David would be the next king. *Exit Samuel, Jesse, and David.* |

## Preparation: Scene 3

*Puppets.*   A group of Israelite soldiers, David with slingshot in belt, David with slingshot in hand, Goliath.

*Props.*   Bread.

*Backdrop.*   A battlefield with Israelite and Philistine soldiers on opposite sides. Research what kind of armor each army may have worn by looking up the story of David in several picture Bibles.


*Enter group of Israelite soldiers.*

| | |
|---|---|
| Narrator | David's brothers were Israelite soldiers for King Saul. One day, Jesse called David in from the fields. He wanted David to take bread to his brothers. They were fighting the Philistines. *Attach bread to David. Enter David from left. Keep him near the left side as he is watching.* |
| Narrator | When David arrived, he saw the Philistines, the enemy, not far off. *Enter Goliath from right.* |
| Narrator | Goliath was the biggest, fiercest soldier, a giant of a man. Each day Goliath challenged the Israelite soldiers. "One of you come and fight me!" he yelled. "If you kill me, then my men will be your slaves. And if I kill you, your men will be our slaves. Come on! Are none of you brave enough to fight me?" Then he laughed. But the Israelite soldiers shuddered. To fight such a huge man would mean certain death! *David walks to center stage.* |
| Narrator | David saw all this. He declared, "I will fight Goliath. God will protect me as he protected me from the lion!" Everyone watched as young David put down the bread. *Exit David with bread. Enter David with slingshot in hand.* |
| Narrator | David took up his slingshot. He walked closer to Goliath. When Goliath saw David, he laughed. "You send a boy to fight me?" Zing! David shot a stone at the giant. It hit him in the head, and he fell down dead. *Goliath falls. Soldiers cheer.* |
| Narrator | It was a great day for the Israelites! *Exit soldiers. David remains.* |
| Narrator | Now you know the beginning of the story of King David. David was one of the greatest leaders of the Jewish people. *Exit David.* |


## For discussion and reflection
What were some of the qualities that helped David be a great leader? Why was David able to defeat Goliath?


## Closing prayer
I bless the Lord who helps me;
even at night God takes care of me.
The Lord is with me all day long;
So I am happy and unafraid.
(based on Psalm 16:7–9)

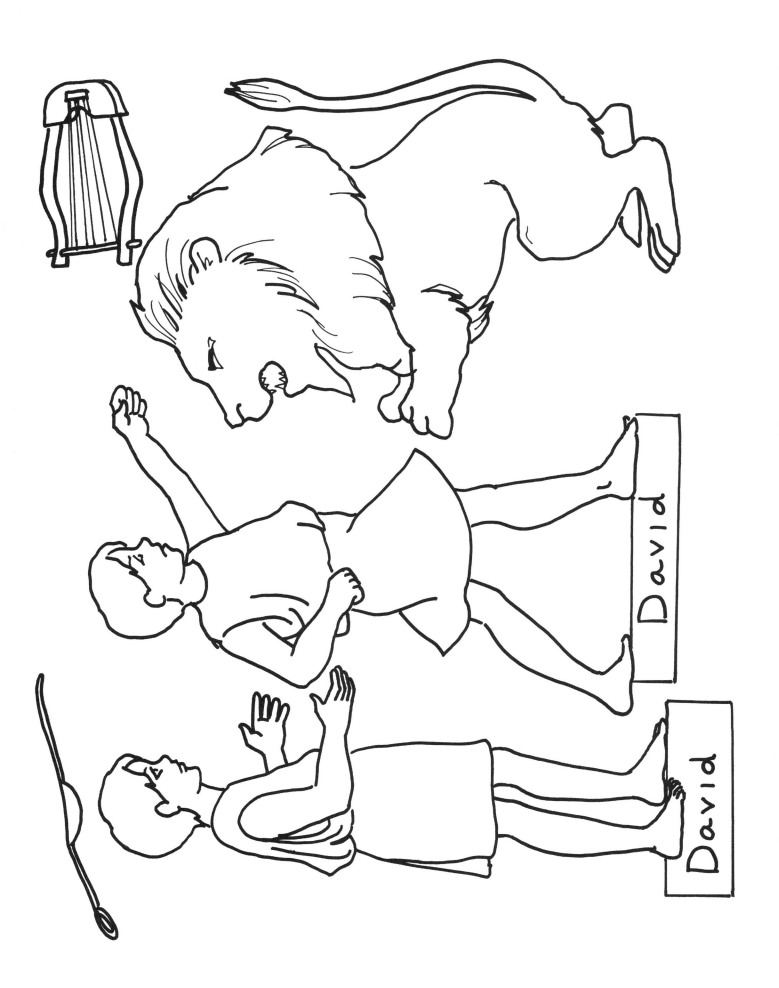

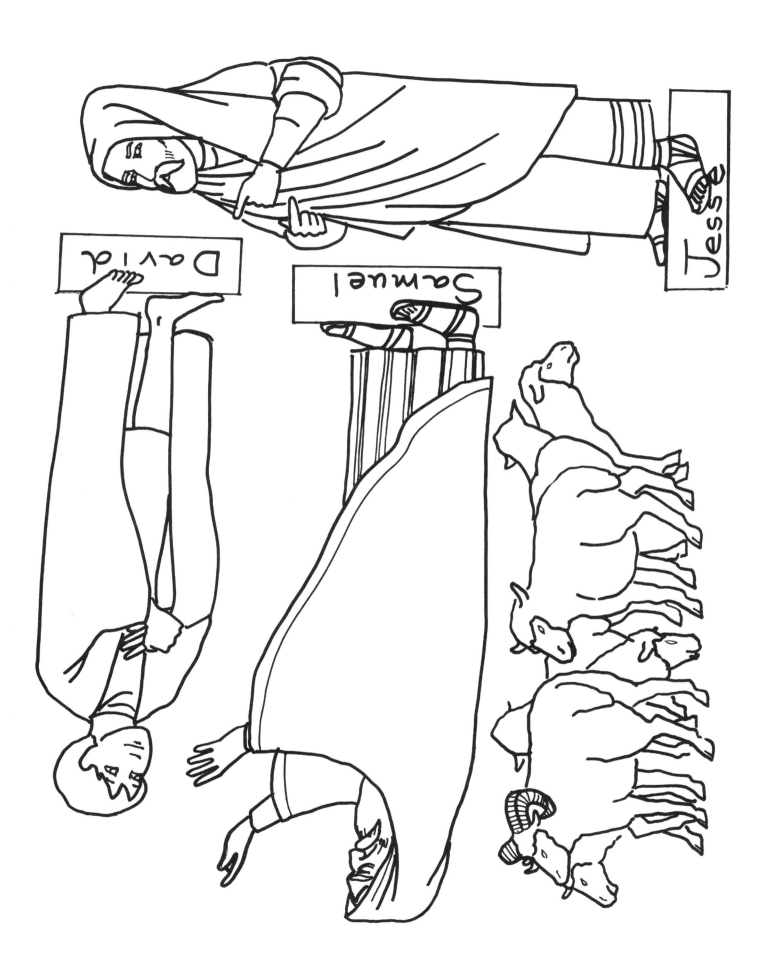

Goliath

# Ravens and a Chariot

*A Story of Elijah*

Based on 1 Kings 17 and 2 Kings 2

## Questions to discuss before the story

Can you name some persons today who teach people about God's love, about peace, and about love for one another? Does everybody agree with them?

## Preparation: Scene 1

*Puppets.*   Elijah with bushy hair, raven with bread, raven with meat.

*Backdrop.*   Poster board on which a cave-like dwelling is drawn on the right side.

*Tips for this scene.*   The sticks can be attached to the top of the ravens and a puppeteer can stand behind and above the backdrop. The ravens can then be moved in such a way that it appears they are flying down to Elijah.

*Narrator enters and stands at the side of the stage.*

| | |
|---|---|
| Narrator | Long ago, there was a holy man named Elijah. *Enter Elijah.* |
| Narrator | God made him a special messenger. Elijah told people what God wanted them to know. Sometimes they would not like what Elijah said, and they'd become angry. Elijah would then need to get out of there! One time, God told him to hide. God would provide food for him. *Elijah walks across the stage to his cave.* |
| Narrator | Now how did God send Elijah food? *Enter raven puppets, flying down to Elijah. They continue to fly around until the scene is over.* |
| Narrator | Every morning and every night, ravens brought him food. Elijah lived in hiding for three years. Then God told him it was time to go to a town. *Exit ravens and Elijah.* |

## Preparation: Scene 2

*Puppets.*   Elijah with bushy hair, mother, child.

*Backdrop.*   A simple home that covers the right half of the poster board. On the left is an outdoor scene.

*Tips for this scene.*   Attach tape to the child puppet so both Elijah and the mother can hold him. A puppeteer will need to reach up to put him into the adults' arms.

*Enter Elijah from the left, walking outside the house.*

| | |
|---|---|
| Narrator | Elijah went around teaching and preaching. *Enter mother and child into the house.* |
| Narrator | He made his home with a poor woman and her young son. *Mother puts child down.* |
| Narrator | One day, Elijah came home and found the mother weeping. *Enter Elijah into the house. Mother bends over child.* |
| Narrator | Her little boy had become very sick and had died just moments before. *Elijah goes over to the child. Mother moves back.* |
| Narrator | Elijah bent over the child. He called out, "O Lord, my God, let this child come back to life!" And God allowed the child to live again! *Child stands up. Elijah picks him up and approaches mother.* |

| Narrator | Elijah carried him to his mother. "See? Your son is alive!" Elijah said. The joyful mother said, "Now indeed I know you are a man of God! God speaks through you!" *Exit all three.* |
|---|---|

## Preparation: Scene 3

*Puppets.* Older Elijah with cloak, Elisha.

*Props.* The water border, which should be copied twice and attached to sticks, and the fiery chariot with horses, also attached to sticks. These will be held as if they were puppets.

*Backdrop.* An outdoor scene

*Tips for this scene.* When Elijah and Elisha come to the River Jordan, raise the two water borders, overlapping in the middle so there is no gap between them. They should be positioned behind Elijah and Elisha. When Elijah strikes the water, move the waters apart to provide an opening for Elijah and Elisha to pass through. The waters then go below and the puppets continue to walk, as if they are now on the other side of the river.

*Enter Elijah.*

| Narrator | Elijah was now getting old. For years he had tried to help people understand God. He met a younger man named Elisha. Elisha would carry on Elijah's work. *Enter Elisha.* |
|---|---|
| Narrator | They both knew it was time for Elijah to go to God. They walked where God told them to go. Elijah and Elisha came to the River Jordan, which had no bridge. *Raise waters from below.* |
| Narrator | Elijah struck the water with his cloak. Look, the water divided! *Move Elijah as if he is striking the water. Open the water borders so the puppets walk through the opening. Close the waters, and take the border below.* |
| Narrator | The two men kept walking. Suddenly, they saw something very bright. *Enter the flaming chariot and horses.* |
| Narrator | It was a chariot pulled by horses. They all seemed to be made of fire! The chariot came closer and Elijah was taken onto it. *Elijah gets on the chariot.* |
| Narrator | Then he was driven off to heaven! *Exit Elijah, the chariot and horses.* |
| Narrator | Elisha watched him go. He never saw Elijah on earth again. But because Elijah did not die, some people believe that Elijah sometimes returns. *Exit Elisha.* |

## For discussion and reflection

What was Elijah's mission or "job" in life? Why do you think some people didn't like what Elijah said? How does God speak to you and me?

## Closing prayer

*Leader:* Dear God, while Elijah was praying, there was a powerful wind but you were not in the wind.

There was an earthquake but you were not in the earthquake.

There was a fire but you were not in the fire.

Then Elijah heard a whisper. You whisper in our hearts. Help us listen.

*All:* Amen.

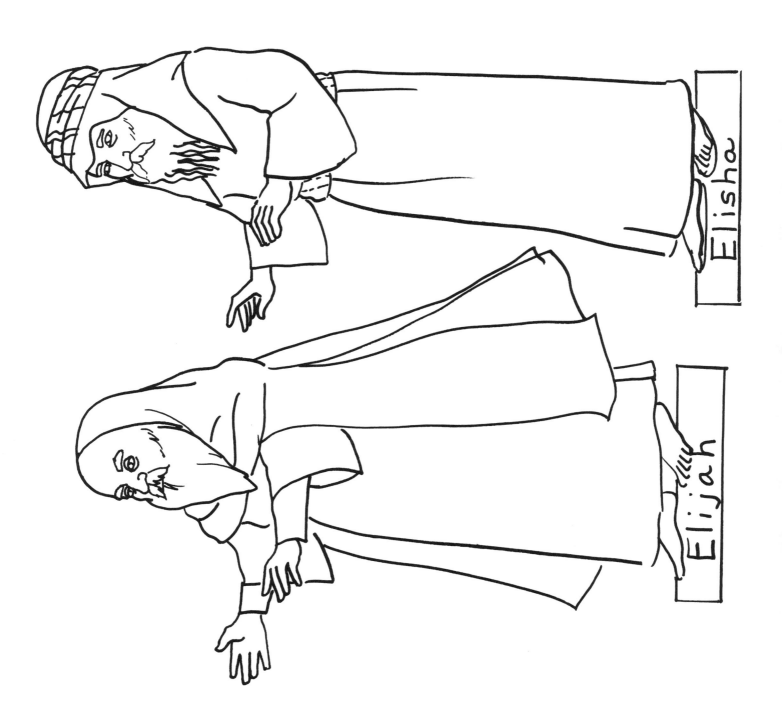

# The Fire and The Angel

## A Story of Shadrach, Meshach, and Abednego

Based on Daniel 3

### Questions to discuss before the story

Have you ever seen a big statue? Is a statue alive? Can a statue walk or talk or help anyone?

### Preparation: Scene 1

*Puppets.*  King, the group of officials standing, officials kneeling, the group of Shadrach, Meshach, and Abednego.

*Props.*  Musical instruments such as bells, maracas, autoharp. Or homemade "instruments": blowing through a comb with waxed paper around it; clapping two wooden sticks together; banging on a pie tin, etc.

*Backdrop.*  A plain in Babylon with a large golden statue to one side.

*Tips for this story.*  Distribute musical instruments to the audience members, explaining that they should keep the instruments quiet until the narrator tells them it is time to play. They should stop when told so the story can go on.

*Narrator stands to the side of the stage. Enter king.*

| | |
|---|---|
| Narrator | Long before Jesus was born, there was a king who was very powerful. But he wanted even more power. So he formed a plan. He had a large statue made of gold. *The king looks the statue over.* |
| Narrator | The king ordered everyone who worked for him to come see the statue. They all came, of course. *Enter group of officials standing.* |
| Narrator | This included three holy men named Shadrach, Meshach, and Abednego. *Enter the group of Shadrach, Meshach, and Abednego.* |
| Narrator | The king announced, "You will hear the sound of the trumpet, flute, harp, bagpipe, and other instruments. Then you must fall down and worship the statue. Anyone who does not do this will be thrown into a huge fire." |
| | *Narrator indicates that audience should play the instruments. Change officials puppet to the group kneeling. Shadrach, Meshach, and Abednego remain standing.* |
| | *Narrator stops the instruments.* |
| Narrator | The king saw that Shadrach, Meshach, and Abednego did not worship the statue. But he gave them another chance. "Be ready now to fall down and worship when you hear the music," the king said. *Audience plays music. Shadrach, Meshach, and Abednego remain standing. Music stops.* |
| Narrator | Shadrach, Meshach, and Abednego said to the king, "We serve only the true God. We will not worship a statue you have made." The king became furious. *King puppet paces angrily across the stage.* |
| Narrator | "Throw them into the fiery furnace!" he ordered. *Exit all the puppets, the officials escorting Shadrach, Meshach, and Abednego.* |

### Preparation: Scene 2

*Puppets.*  Shadrach, Meshach, and Abednego, angel, king, group of officials standing.

*Props.* A border that looks like fire, colored in fiery colors. Attach it to the front of the right side of the stage.

*Backdrop.* Draw or paint an entire poster board to look like a raging fire.

*Enter Shadrach, Meshach, and Abednego behind the fire border. It appears that they walk around in the fire.*

Narrator    The king had Shadrach, Meshach, and Abednego thrown into a fiery furnace. But they were not hurt! And they were not alone, either. *Enter the angel who walks around in the fire with the men.*

Narrator    The three men and the angel walked around in the fire. They prayed, "Blessed are you, O Lord, the God of our fathers and mothers. You are above all others. We praise you forever! Angels of the Lord, bless the Lord! Sun and moon, bless the Lord! Waters and rain, bless the Lord! Birds of the air and creatures of the sea and land, bless the Lord! All people, bless the Lord and give him thanks and praise!" *Enter king and officials from the left, standing near the fire border, but not in it. Angel and Shadrach, Meshach, and Abednego continue to walk in the fire.*

Narrator    Now the king arrived at the furnace. He was amazed at what he saw. No one was hurt! Shadrach, Meshach, and Abednego were praying! And there was a fourth figure with them! The king said to the officials, "Did I not order three men to be thrown into the fire? I see a fourth, an angel sent by their God to protect them!" The king walked closer to the fire. He called out, "Come out, you men of the most high God!" *Angel exits below. Shadrach, Meshach, and Abednego come out from behind the fire border.*

Narrator    Shadrach, Meshach and Abednego came out of the fire. The king looked them over. "You are not hurt at all! Not a hair on your heads has burned, nor any of your clothing! You do not even smell of smoke! Blessed is this God of yours, who sent an angel to deliver you from the flames. You accepted death rather than worship a false god. Your God saved you. We must all praise your God, for he is the one, true God!" *Audience plays music. Exit all the puppets.*

## For discussion and reflection

What is the first commandment of God? Why wouldn't Shadrach, Meshach, and Abednego bow down to the statue? How do we honor and worship God?

## Closing prayer

*Leader:* Blessed are you, O Lord, the God of our fathers and mothers.

*All:* We praise you forever!

*Leader:* With all your angels we bless you. With the sun and the moon, we bless you.

*All:* We praise you forever!

*Leader:* With the the birds of the air and all your creatures we bless you.

*All:* We praise you forever!

*Leader:* With all peoples of the earth we bless you, Lord.

*All:* We praise you forever! Amen.

Officials

King

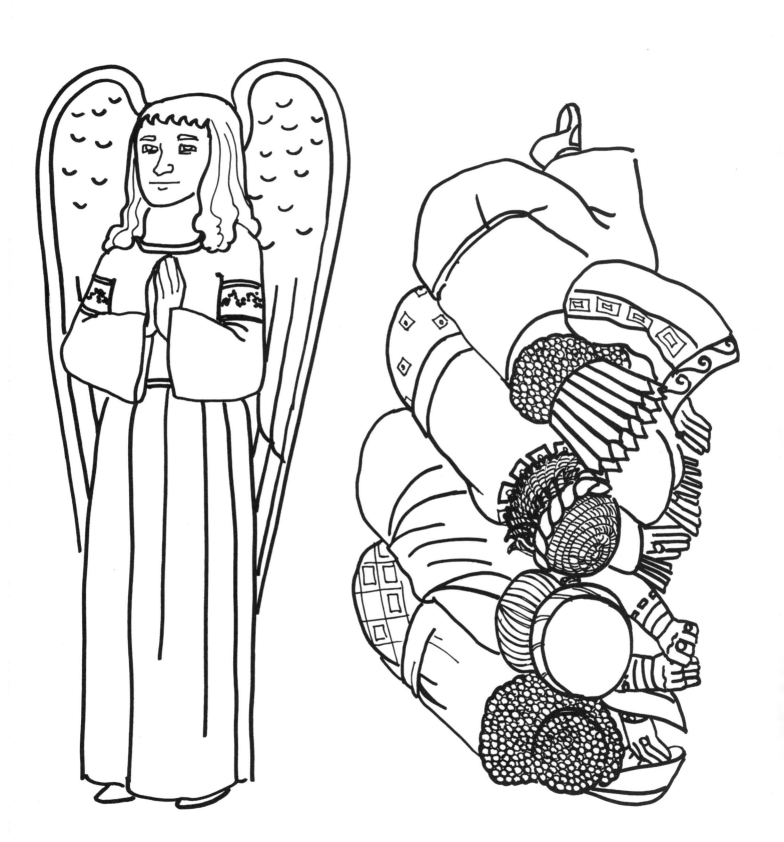

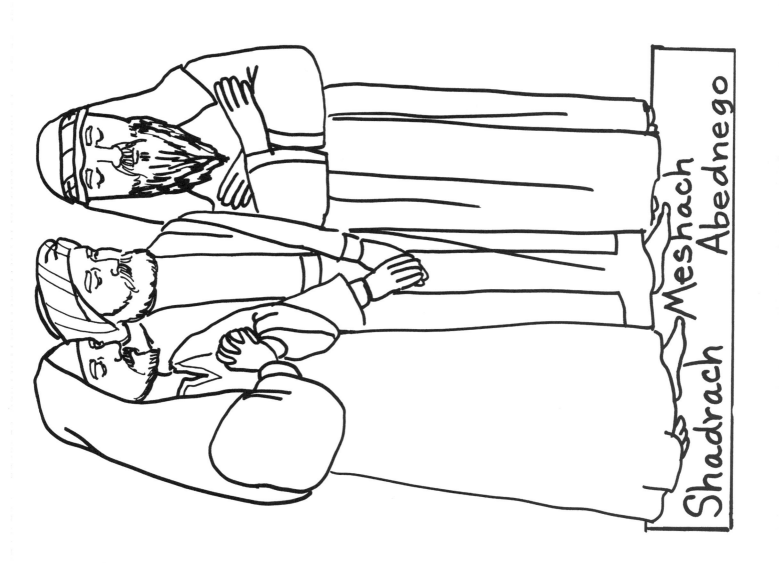

# Running from God, Turning to God

*A Story of Jonah*

Based on the book of Jonah

## Questions to discuss before the story

Did you ever want to run away from something or someone? Why?

## Preparation: Scene 1

*Puppets.*  The large Jonah with hand at mouth, and the small Jonah.

*Props.*  The ship and sailors, and the water strip.

*Backdrop.*  A harbor scene.

*Tips for this scene.*  Jonah can be rather comical. You might also add sound effects for the storm: for example, have the audience make a wind sound by blowing through pursed lips; or the sound of rain with a rain stick (see the story of Noah for directions), etc.

*Narrator stands to the side of the stage.*

| | |
|---|---|
| Narrator | Once there was a man named Jonah. *Enter the large Jonah.* |
| Narrator | God spoke to him. "Jonah, go to the large city of Nineveh," God said. "There is much wickedness there. Preach to the people. Tell them I know of their evil ways." *Jonah paces back and forth across the stage.* |
| Narrator | Now Jonah thought about this job. "Those people don't want to hear that!" Jonah thought. "If they are so evil, they might even harm me!" Jonah did not go to Nineveh. In fact, he went as fast as he could in the opposite direction. Jonah thought he could run away from God. But he would find out he was wrong. *Exit Jonah. Enter the ship and sailors puppet. Enter the small Jonah.* |
| Narrator | Jonah went to a port town and boarded a ship. *The small Jonah gets on the ship.* |
| Narrator | Soon, God sent a huge wind upon the sea. The ship was tossed about by great waves. This frightened the sailors very much. *Rock ship from side to side.* |
| Narrator | "This is my fault," Jonah shouted. "I am running away from God." "What shall we do?" the sailors cried. "Throw me overboard," Jonah said. "That's the only way to stop this storm." None of the sailors wanted to do this. But the sea was getting more dangerous by the minute. *Rock the boat more wildly.* |
| Narrator | The sailors prayed for forgiveness. Then they threw Jonah into the sea. *The Jonah puppet goes overboard. Lay him sideways behind the water strip.* |
| Narrator | Down went Jonah and the water quieted! *The boat settles down, the sailors and boat sail to the edge of the stage and exit. Jonah bobs up and down, appearing and disappearing behind the water strip. Change backdrop for scene 2.* |

## Preparation: Scene 2

*Puppets.*  Jonah swallowed, Jonah in fish, and the big fish.

*Props.*  The water strip.

*Backdrop.*  Blue with an underwater scene, such as fish and plants on the bottom two-thirds of the poster board. The top third should be sky with a bit of shoreline on one side.

*Tips for this scene.* The big fish should move up and down behind the water strip, with Jonah moving up and down inside the fish.

| | |
|---|---|
| Narrator | So there was Jonah, about to drown. *Jonah swallowed bobs up and down behind the water strip.* |
| Narrator | But even underwater, he couldn't lose God. God sent a large fish to swallow Jonah! *Have the fish swim by and bring the Jonah puppet up from below right into the fish. Jonah must stay on the audience side of the fish.* |
| Narrator | For three days and three nights, Jonah lived in the belly of that fish. *Optional: Switch Jonah swallowed to Jonah praying.* |
| Narrator | Jonah prayed. Then God had the fish spit Jonah out onto land. *The fish swims up to the shore line. Jonah comes out of the fish. The fish swims back down, and exits below.* |
| Narrator | "Now," God said. "Go to Nineveh and I will tell you what to say." This time, Jonah set out in the right direction for Nineveh. *Exit Jonah. Take down water strip, and change the backdrop.* |

## Preparation: Scene 3

*Puppets.* Jonah in Nineveh, the people of Nineveh, the king.
*Backdrop.* A rich city.

*Enter Jonah in Nineveh. He walks slowly across the stage.*

| | |
|---|---|
| Narrator | Jonah arrived in Nineveh and began shouting, "In forty days, Nineveh will be destroyed. God is upset by your selfish, violent ways!" *Jonah stops, looking around.* |
| Narrator | Then he looked about fearfully. No one came to laugh at him or hurt him. No one even yelled at him! Instead, they believed him. *Enter people of Nineveh.* |
| Narrator | The people of Nineveh put on clothing called sackcloth to show that they were sorry. They wanted to change their ways. When the king heard this, he put on sackcloth too. *Enter the king. The people come to him. Jonah watches.* |
| Narrator | "Let us fast from food and change how we live. Then maybe God will give us another chance," the king said. And that is exactly what happened. God forgave them. God did not destroy Nineveh. *Exit king and people.* |
| Narrator | So there was Jonah, standing in a happier Nineveh. He had done his job well. But Jonah wasn't satisfied. In fact, he was angry with God. *Jonah paces.* |
| Narrator | "When you first told me to do this," Jonah said to God, "I didn't want to. I knew you are a merciful God. I knew you would forgive them! And I was right. I am angry. Very angry. I don't think you should have saved them!" "Jonah," said God. "Do you have a reason to be angry? Shouldn't I care about all the people and animals, and forgive them?" *Jonah exits silently. Narrator comes to stand in front of the stage.* |
| Narrator | God asked Jonah to go to Nineveh. God asked the people of Nineveh to change their ways. God was loving and gentle with Jonah and the other people. God is loving and gentle with us, too. |

## For discussion and reflection

Why did God send Jonah to Nineveh? Why didn't God just destroy the city? Does God always give us another chance?

## Closing prayer

(Give each child a colorful index card with a Scripture quote on it.)
*Leader:* Dear God, you tell us, "You shall put these words of mine in your heart and soul." Help us think about these words and keep them in our hearts.
*All:* Amen.

Jonah

Jonah in Fish

Jonah is Swallowed

Jonah in Nineveh

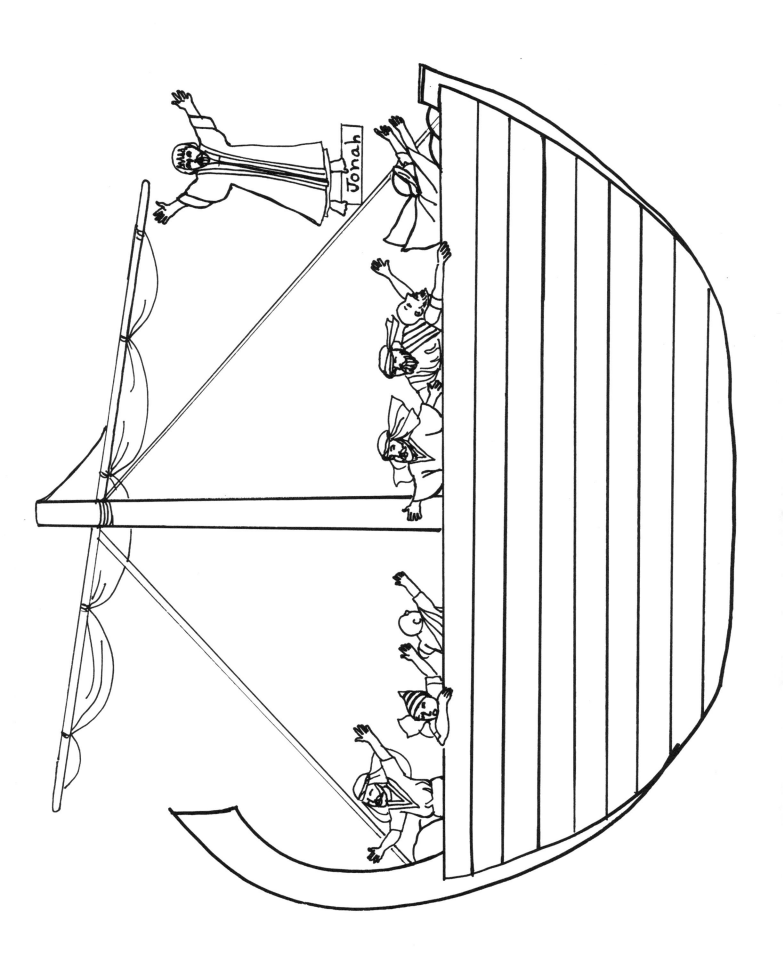

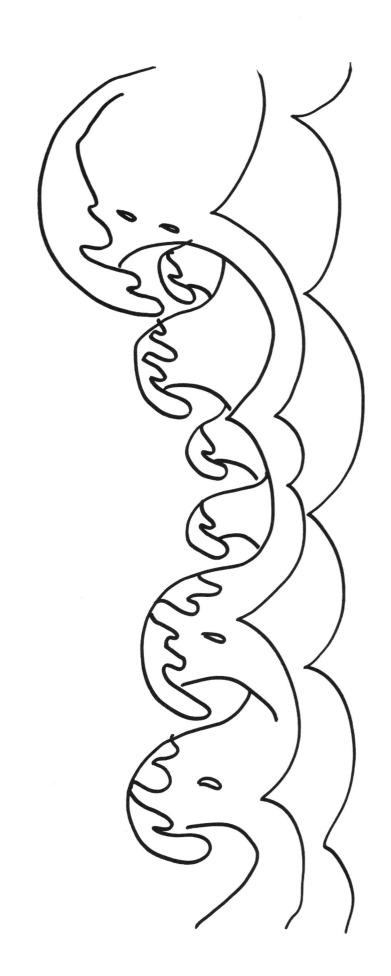

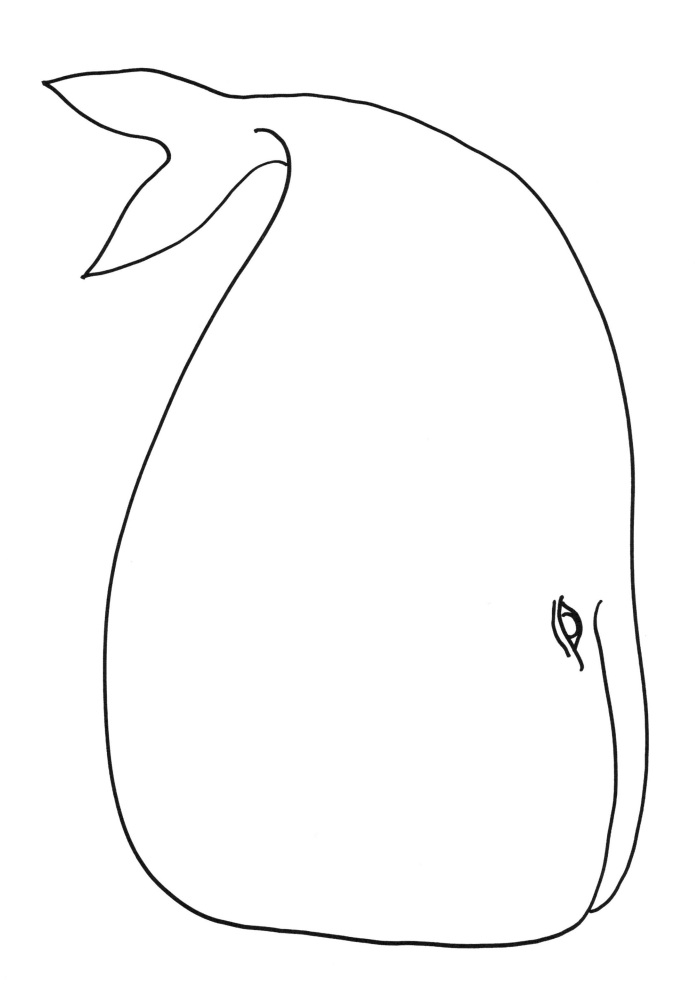

People of Nineveh

King of Nineveh

# Speechless with Joy

## A Story of John the Baptist

Based on Luke 1:5–25, 57–80

**Questions to discuss before the story**

Have you ever prayed really hard for something? What happened?

**Preparation: Scene 1**

*Puppets.* Zechariah, Gabriel, a group of people praying in the temple.

*Backdrop.* The backdrop must be the temple. About two-thirds of the drawing is the sanctuary containing an incense burner. The rest, indicated by a vertical line for a wall, can be another room in the temple where the others pray as Zechariah burns the incense.

*Tips for this scene.* Zechariah is understandably unnerved when Gabriel appears. Have him act startled and befuddled. If it is feasible, a real incense burner could be set up on a small table next to the stage. The narrator could light some incense when Zechariah is in the sanctuary.

*The narrator stands in front of the stage.*

| | |
|---|---|
| Narrator | Long ago, about two thousand years ago, there lived a couple named Zechariah and Elizabeth. They were good people. They honored God and obeyed the commandments. And God loved them. However, Elizabeth and Zechariah had one great sadness in their life. They didn't have any children. They had hoped, and they had prayed for a child. Now they were too old to have a baby. *The narrator moves to the side and Zechariah enters at one side of the stage, where he stands still.* |
| Narrator | Zechariah was a priest in the Jewish religion. Sometimes he was at the temple. One day, it was his turn to burn incense. Other people prayed in another part of the temple. *Enter the praying people into their section.* |
| Narrator | Zechariah quietly entered the sanctuary. That was the holiest part of the temple. *Zechariah approaches the incense burner.* |
| Narrator | He was all alone, or so he thought. *Enter Gabriel from below. Zechariah jumps in fear.* |
| Narrator | Without warning, a magnificent angel appeared. The angel said, "Do not be afraid, Zechariah, for your prayers have been answered. You and Elizabeth will have a son! You shall name him John. That means 'God has shown favor.' John will become great in the eyes of God. Your son will be a prophet like Elijah. He will bring many people to God." |
| Narrator | Now Zechariah was astonished. First an angel, and now this news! He said, "How can I know that something so impossible will come true?" The angel answered, "I am Gabriel the archangel who stands before God. I was sent to give you this good news. But since you doubt it, you won't be able to talk anymore until all this takes place." Then without another word, Gabriel disappeared. *Exit Gabriel below. Zechariah moves to the other part of the temple, joining the praying people.* |
| Narrator | Zechariah left the sanctuary and joined the others. The people asked, "What took you so long?" But Zechariah could not tell them. He could not talk at all. "What's wrong?" the others asked. "Are you all right?" But Zechariah remained speechless. The people realized that he must have had a vision in the sanctuary. Silently, Zechariah went home. *Exit Zechariah, then exit the others.* |

## Preparation: Scene 2

*Puppets.*  Elizabeth and infant John, Zechariah, neighbors.

*Props.*  Tablet with two-sided tape on it.

*Backdrop.*  Two-thirds of the backdrop should be the inside of Elizabeth and Zechariah's home. Draw a bold vertical line to indicate the outside wall. The space on the other side of the wall will be the outdoors, where the neighbors arrive and come to the "door."

*The narrator stands in front of the stage.*

| | |
|---|---|
| Narrator | Now everything came to pass just as the angel Gabriel had said. Elizabeth must have been puzzled at first that Zechariah could not speak. But she was overjoyed that she would at last become a mother. *The narrator steps to the side of the stage. Enter Elizabeth with baby John. She walks about the house. The neighbors enter from the side, to stand at the door.* |
| Narrator | "Zechariah!" Elizabeth called, as she cradled her newborn baby in her arms. "All of our neighbors have come to celebrate our son!" *Enter Zechariah from below. He answers the door, and the neighbors walk in. They stand behind Elizabeth and John.* |
| Narrator | "Will you will name him Zechariah, after his father?" one of the neighbors asked Elizabeth. Zechariah looked on silently, but Elizabeth smiled. "No," she said. "He will be called John." Now the neighbors were very surprised. Parents usually named their children after someone else in their family! Another neighbor piped up. "None of your relatives are named John. Is this the name you want, Zechariah?" Zechariah asked for a tablet to write his answer. *Exit Zechariah below, place the tablet on the puppet, and reenter Zechariah.* |
| Narrator | On the tablet he wrote, "John is his name." Immediately, Zechariah could talk! He began praising God and talking about John's future. *Zechariah begins moving about the stage joyfully.* |
| Narrator | "You, child, will be called a prophet of God. You will go before the Lord and prepare his way." As the neighbors left, they murmured, "What will this child be? This is so amazing!" *Exit neighbors.* |
| Narrator | Zechariah kept talking about the greatness of God. *Zechariah continues to move about the stage.* |
| Narrator | Elizabeth smiled down at the special baby in her arms. *Exit both puppets. The narrator moves in front of the stage.* |
| Narrator | John grew up to be a great prophet. He prepared the way for the Lord Jesus. |

## For discussion and reflection

What were Zechariah and Elizabeth praying for? Does God always give us what we pray for? Does God know better than we do what is good for us?

## Closing prayer

*Leader:* John's father said, "And you, child, shall be called the prophet of the Most High; for you will go before the Lord to prepare his ways." As God called John to prepare the way for Jesus, so God calls you (child's name) to follow Jesus.

(As each child's name is called, that child approaches the leader who signs the child's forehead with a cross.)

Zechariah

יוֹחָנָן

Gabriel the Archangel

Praying People

Neighbors

Elizabeth

# In Search of a King

## A Story of the Wise Men

Based on Matthew 2:1–12

### Questions to discuss before the story

Did you ever travel to a special place or to visit someone you hadn't seen for a long time? What did you think about while you were traveling?

### Preparation: Scene 1

*Puppets.* The wise men and the camel.

*Props.* The star, which should be on a stick long enough so that it can held up like a puppet but can be in the "sky." It should be decorated beautifully.

*Backdrop.* The area which the wise men traveled through before they reached Jerusalem was probably the Mideast. They may have traveled through deserts, sandy coastal plains, and mountains. Portray some of these areas on the backdrop.

*The narrator stands to the side of the stage.*

| | |
|---|---|
| Narrator | When Jesus was born in Bethlehem, a brilliant star shone in the sky. *The star rises on one side of the stage.* |
| Narrator | Far away from Bethlehem lived some wise men. They studied a great deal about many subjects. *Enter the three wise men on the other side.* |
| Narrator | The wise men saw the star. They knew the star meant that a special baby was born. This child would someday be a leader of the Jewish people. Each of these men wanted to find and honor this baby. So they left their families and homes and all that was familiar to them to travel in search of Jesus. *Enter the camel. The wise men, with the camel following, walk slowly toward the other side of the stage.* |
| Narrator | They didn't know exactly where the child king would be born. But they decided to follow the star until they found the child. It was going to be a long journey. |

### Preparation: Scene 2

*Puppets.* The wise men, the camel, King Herod, and chief priest and scribes.

*Props.* The star.

*Backdrop.* Herod's palace, which should be centered on the backdrop, with "outside" (Jerusalem) on either side of the palace.

*Enter the wise men and the camel, pausing outside the palace.*

| | |
|---|---|
| Narrator | After traveling for many weeks, the wise men came to the great city of Jerusalem. There they lost sight of the star they had followed for so long. In this city lived the king. *Enter King Herod from below. His throne should in the center of the palace.* |
| Narrator | The wise men went to the king's palace. They asked where they might find the baby who would become king. *The wise men approach Herod in his palace, the camel exits below.* |
| Narrator | Now King Herod was a wicked man. He did not want any new king to take his place. When the wise men told him about the star and the baby, he was worried. He called for the chief |

priest and scribes. *Wise men move back but stay in the palace. Enter chief priest and scribes from below. They approach Herod.*

Narrator   King Herod asked them if they knew anything about a child who would become king of the Jews. "The prophets have written that this child would be born in Bethlehem," they told the king. *Exit the chief priest and scribes below. The wise men remain where they are while Herod ponders.*

Narrator   King Herod pretended he was delighted to hear about this baby. But he really meant to harm Jesus. He called the wise men back to him. *The wise men approach the king.*

Narrator   The king said, "You will find this child in a small town called Bethlehem. When you find him, come back to tell me. Then I can go to honor him, too." *The wise men give a little bow and walk toward the other side of the stage, away from Herod.*

Narrator   So the wise men set out. *The camel enters from below, where the wise men are now.*

Narrator   As they left Jerusalem, once again they saw the star. *The star rises, the wise men pause.*

Narrator   Overjoyed, they journeyed on. *They exit.*

## Preparation: Scene 3

*Puppets.*   The wise men, Mary and baby Jesus, and an angel.

*Props.*   Gold, frankincense, and myrrh, with two-sided tape on the back.

*Backdrop.*   A little house in Bethlehem on the left side; on the right side, an inn where the wise men will stay at night. Draw a star similar to the one used earlier over the little house.

*Tips for this scene.*   Attach the stick on the angel so it can be lowered down from above the backdrop.


*Mary and Jesus enter from below into the little house on the backdrop. Enter wise men from left.*

Narrator   The wise men traveled on to Bethlehem. There the star led them to Mary and Baby Jesus. At last, the wise men had found the one they had sought for so long! The Christ Child, the King of kings! Happily, they bowed down to honor him. They gave the child gifts of gold, frankincense, and myrrh. *The wise men bow a little, and remain there for a brief time. A puppeteer reaches up to stick the gifts onto the backdrop. Mary and Jesus remain on stage in the house, but the wise men then move on to the next building.*

Narrator   Later, an angel came to the wise men in a dream. *Enter angel from above.*

Narrator   The angel warned them not to go back to Herod. *Exit angel from above.*

Narrator   And so they returned home a different way. *Exit wise men. Exit Mary and Jesus.*

Narrator   Jesus was loved, protected, and taught well by his parents. As he grew, he became wise and loving.

## For discussion and reflection

Why were the wise men willing to make such a long journey so far from their homes? What do you do to prepare to celebrate Jesus' birth?

## Closing prayer

*Leader:* Like the wise men, we choose to travel to Jesus. Picture yourself walking or running, excited that you will see Jesus. (Pause) Along the way, you become lost, losing sight of where you want to go. Picture yourself stopping, looking around. (Pause) You meet someone like King Herod. You must find the right way again. (Pause) Then like the wise men, you find your way to Jesus.

*All:* Jesus is here. Amen!

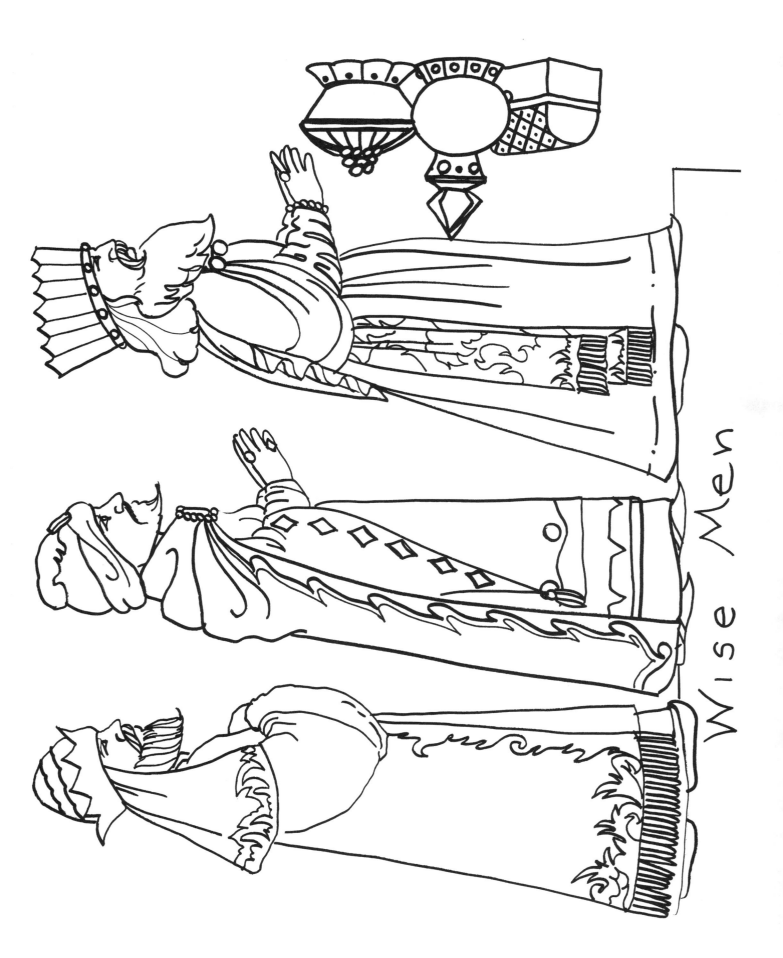

Wise Men

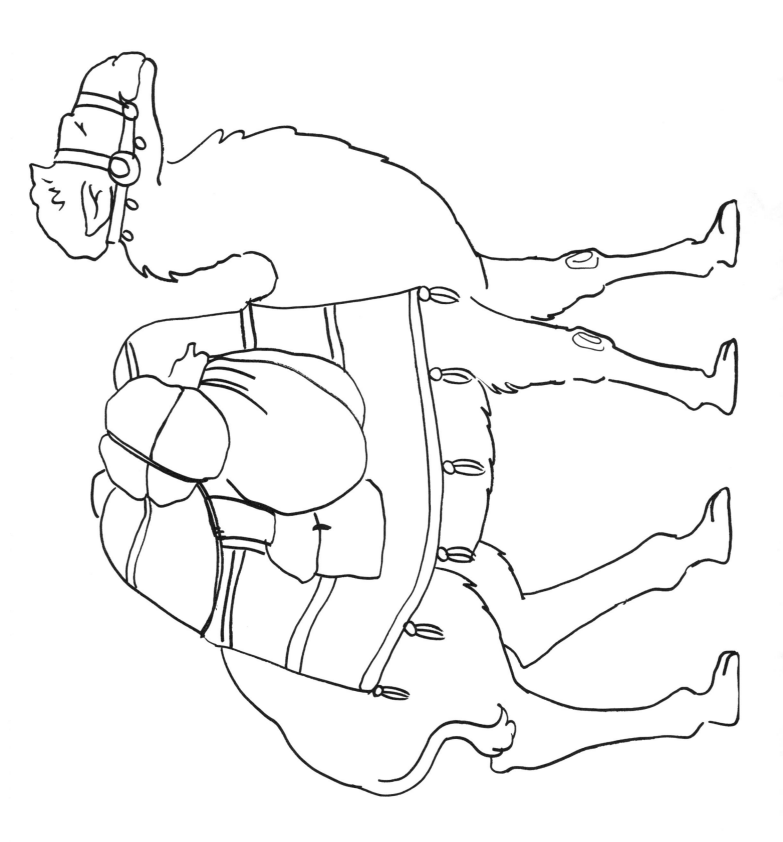

Herod

Mary and Baby Jesus

Chief Priest and Scribes

# Jesus the Storyteller

*The Parables of the Lost Sheep,*
*the Prodigal Son,*
*and the Good Samaritan*  Based on Luke 15:4–7; Luke 15:11–32, and Luke 10:25–37

## Questions to discuss before the story

Have you ever lost something very special to you? How did you feel? Did you try to find it?

## Preparation: Scene 1

*Puppets.* The shepherd and the lost lamb.

*Props.* A border of sheep to represent the ninety-nine sheep who do not stray. Attach it to the front of the stage so the shepherd can walk behind it, looking for the lost one.

*Backdrop.* The backdrop is the same for all three scenes. Draw a mountainside where people have gathered. Jesus is seated in a prominent place, children cluster around him, and adults sit and stand nearby, listening.

*The narrator stands next to the stage, and gestures toward the backdrop.*

| | |
|---|---|
| Narrator | As Jesus was growing up, he came to understand that he was God's Son. He also knew that he was on earth to teach others about God. Jesus wanted us to know how much God loves us. He taught that God asks us to treat others fairly and lovingly. Jesus was a great storyteller. Here are two of his stories that teach us about God's great love. The first is called "The Lost Sheep." *A puppeteer attaches the sheep border to the front of the stage.* |
| Narrator | Once there was a shepherd (*enter shepherd*) who took great care of his sheep. He had a flock of one hundred sheep. One day, as the shepherd walked among his sheep, he noticed a lamb was missing. He searched and searched for the lamb, but he could not find it there with the others. So he left the flock. *A puppeteer pulls the sheep border down.* |
| Narrator | He went off into the wilderness to look for the one lamb. *Shepherd walks from one end of the stage to the other, comes back to the center, and goes below briefly so the lamb can be attached to his shoulders.* |
| Narrator | After a long search, the shepherd found the lamb! *Enter the shepherd and the lamb at one side of the stage.* |
| Narrator | He carried the lamb on his shoulders. He rejoiced all the way home. *They walk across the stage.* |
| Narrator | Then he called his friends and neighbors to come and celebrate with him. At the end of the story Jesus talks to us. He says that there is much joy in heaven when one person comes back to God's love. *Exit the shepherd and sheep. The narrator initiates a brief discussion with the audience.* |

## Preparation: Scene 2

*Puppets.* The younger son, the father, the older son, pigs.

*Props.* Ragged clothing for the younger son, attached like paper doll clothing, and similarly, a richly decorated robe; small confetti and glitter.

| Narrator | Jesus' second story about God's great love is called "The Prodigal Son." There once was a man with two sons. They had a good life. They had everything that they needed. *Enter father, younger son, and older son. Younger son approaches the father, older son stays off to one side.* |
|---|---|
| Narrator | One day, the younger son said to his father: "Father, give me my share of our property." And the father did. *Exit father and older son.* |
| Narrator | Soon, the young man sold his property. He took the money and traveled to a distant land. There he lived in a wild, reckless way. *Younger son races around the stage, jumping. Drop confetti from over the backdrop.* |
| Narrator | Soon, however, he ran out of money. He needed a job and he found one, tending pigs. *Exit younger son. Place ragged clothing on him. He then enters with the pigs on one side of the stage.* |
| Narrator | While he had to feed the pigs, he did not have any food for himself. He was miserable. One day he came to his senses. "My father's hired servants have plenty to eat. Here I am, starving." he said. "I'll go home. I'll tell my father I'm sorry. I'll work for him as a hired servant." So he set off for home. *Exit pigs. Younger son starts to walk across the stage.* |
| Narrator | While the son was still a long way off, his father saw him coming. The father ran to him. *Enter father from the other side.* |
| Narrator | He embraced his son. "Father," the young man said, "I have sinned against God and against you. I am not worthy to be called your son." But the happy father ordered a party to celebrate his son's return. "Bring him fine clothes! Prepare a great feast! My son was dead, and has come back to life!" he exclaimed. *Exit younger son. Take off the ragged clothing and replace it with the robe. Enter older son who approaches the father.* |
| Narrator | The older son heard about his brother's return and about the party. He was hurt and angry. "I've worked hard for you all my life," he said to his father. "I've always done what you told me to do. Yet you never gave me a party like this. My brother comes back after living foolishly, and you give him a party!" The father looked at him with love. "My son," he said, "you are always with me. Everything I own is yours also. But today we must celebrate. Your brother was dead and now he is alive. He was lost to us and now is found!" *Enter younger son in new clothing. The father and both sons do a little dance across the stage. Sprinkle glitter from the top. Exit all puppets.* |

## Preparation: Scene 3

*Puppets.* Injured man, a priest, a Levite, a Samaritan.

| Narrator | In the Bible, we are taught to love God with all our heart and strength. And we are to love our neighbor as we love ourselves. One day a man asked Jesus who our neighbors are. And Jesus answered with the story of "The Good Samaritan." One day, he said, a Jewish man was traveling from Jerusalem to Jericho. Some robbers hurt him and stole his money. *Enter the injured man from below to lie on the center of the stage.* |
|---|---|
| Narrator | Now along this same road came a Jewish priest. *Enter priest.* |
| Narrator | You would expect someone like him to be kind and loving toward the injured man. But no— he walked around the man and went on his way. *The priest moves as close to the backdrop as possible and exits the other side.* |
| Narrator | Sometime later, a Levite, who was like a priest, came along. He too walked on by. *Enter the Levite who walks around the injured man.* |
| Narrator | Then along came a man from the country of Samaria. *Enter the Samaritan who walks over closely to the injured man.* |

| Narrator | The Jews and the Samaritans were enemies, so no one would expect a Samaritan to help a Jewish person. But he did. *The Samaritan leans over the man.* |
| Narrator | The Samaritan put medicine and bandages on him. Then he helped the injured man up. *The Samaritan "helps" the injured man up.* |
| Narrator | The Samaritan took the injured man to an inn. There he cared for the man himself. The next day he paid the innkeeper and said: "Take care of this man. If you spend more than this, I will repay you later." *They exit together as the Samaritan "supports" the injured man.* |
| Narrator | If Jesus were telling you this story today, he would ask you, "Who was the neighbor to the injured man?" *The narrator lets audience respond.* |
| Narrator | Now Jesus would tell you, "Go and do the same." *Narrator exits.* |

## For discussion and reflection

Why was there so much celebration at the end of the first two stories? How do you feel when you've done something wrong and then said you're sorry? Does God always forgive us?

## Closing prayer

Jesus, our great teacher, help us forgive one another as you forgive us. Show us the way to heaven, so we can follow you.

*All:* Amen.

Shepherd

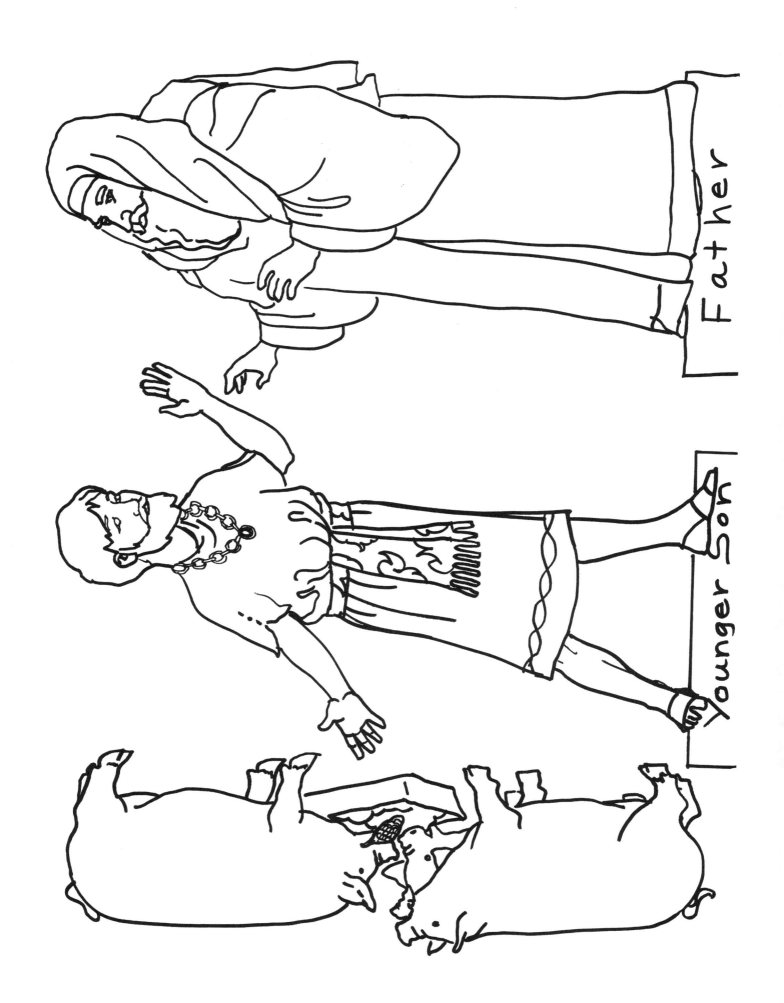

Father

Younger Son

Older Son

Samaritan

Priest

Levite

# Loaves, Fish, and a Big Wind

## A Story of Two Miracles

Based on Matthew 14:13–33

### Questions to discuss before the story

*Story 1*—Have you ever been really hungry? What did you do?

*Story 2*—Have you ever been in a boat? What was it like?

### Preparation: Scene 1

*Puppets.* Jesus sitting, two disciples, and a crowd.

*Props.* Five loaves and two fish, with two-sided tape on the back. Also, a real basket or two, filled with French or pita bread and fish-shaped crackers, more than enough to feed everyone in the audience.

*Backdrop.* A sunny day on a hillside. Draw people who are listening to Jesus (but do not draw Jesus), some further off, others closer.

*The narrator stands next to the stage. Enter Jesus sitting, crowd, and disciples.*

| Narrator | Jesus had been teaching large crowds all day. He knew the people were very hungry. "Give these people some food," Jesus told his disciples. They looked out at the huge numbers of people. "We only have five loaves of bread and two fish," one of the disciples said. "That won't begin to feed all these people!" "Bring the food to me," Jesus said. *A puppeteer reaches up and tapes the bread and fish onto Jesus' hands.* |
|---|---|
| Narrator | Jesus took the loaves and fish. He looked up to heaven and he said the blessing. Then he broke the loaves, and handed them out. There was more than enough to feed everyone! *Exit all the puppets. The narrator then brings out the baskets of bread and fish crackers, and invites someone to say a blessing. Then the narrator passes the baskets for everyone to share the food.* |

### Preparation: Scene 2

*Puppets.* The boat with the disciples, Peter, Jesus standing.

*Props.* The water border.

*Backdrop.* Use a poster board color that shows it is nighttime but is light enough to draw on. The bottom portion of the backdrop can be water and a shoreline. A mountain should be in the background. The water border should be copied enough times to span the front of the stage. Attach it onto the front of the stage so the boat will "float" behind it.

*Tips for this scene.* Peter should be attached to the boat with two-sided tape so he can be taken off the boat to walk on water.

*The narrator stands in front of the stage.*

| Narrator | After the crowd of people had eaten and were satisfied, they left. Jesus told his disciples to get into their boat. They would row to the other side of the water. He would come later. Jesus then went up the mountain to pray. *The narrator moves to the side of the stage. Enter the boat with the disciples and Peter, who must also be in the boat. The boat should remain on one side of the stage.* |
|---|---|

| | |
|---|---|
| Narrator | Evening came on. A strong wind came up on the water. The waves tossed the boat about. *The audience can make wind sounds by blowing through pursed lips. Begin rocking the boat. Stop the wind sounds.* |
| Narrator | Suddenly, they saw a figure coming toward them. The person was not in a boat, but was walking on the water! *Enter Jesus, walking slowly across the water. His feet should show just above the water border.* |
| Narrator | The disciples were terrified. "It's a ghost!" they cried out. The figure immediately called, "Take courage! It is I, Jesus! Don't be afraid." Peter called back, "Lord, if it is really you, tell me to walk over the water to you." Jesus said to come. *Peter jumps into the water. Walk him along the border. He can bob up and down just slightly.* |
| Narrator | Peter jumped out of the boat and began walking. Peter the fisherman was actually walking on top of the water! *Peter and Jesus are moving closer to each other. Audience can briefly make wind sounds.* |
| Narrator | But Peter felt how strong the wind was. He became afraid. As soon as he felt afraid, he began to sink. *Peter sinks behind the border up to his waist. Jesus should now be close to him.* |
| Narrator | Immediately, Jesus reached out and caught him. *Jesus pulls Peter up.* |
| Narrator | They both stood on the water. Jesus said to Peter, "Do not doubt me. Trust me." Jesus and Peter got into the boat. *Both puppets board the boat.* |
| Narrator | Then the wind died down. *The boat stops rocking.* |
| Narrator | The disciples looked at Jesus and said, "You surely are the Son of God!" *Exit all puppets.* |

## For discussion and reflection

Story 1—Why did Jesus want the loaves and fish? Does God take care of us? How?

Story 2—Why was Peter afraid? Will Jesus help us if we trust him?

## Closing prayer

Jesus, you are the bread of life. Help us to believe in you, to trust you, and to love you always.

*All:* Amen.

Jesus

Disciples

Crowd

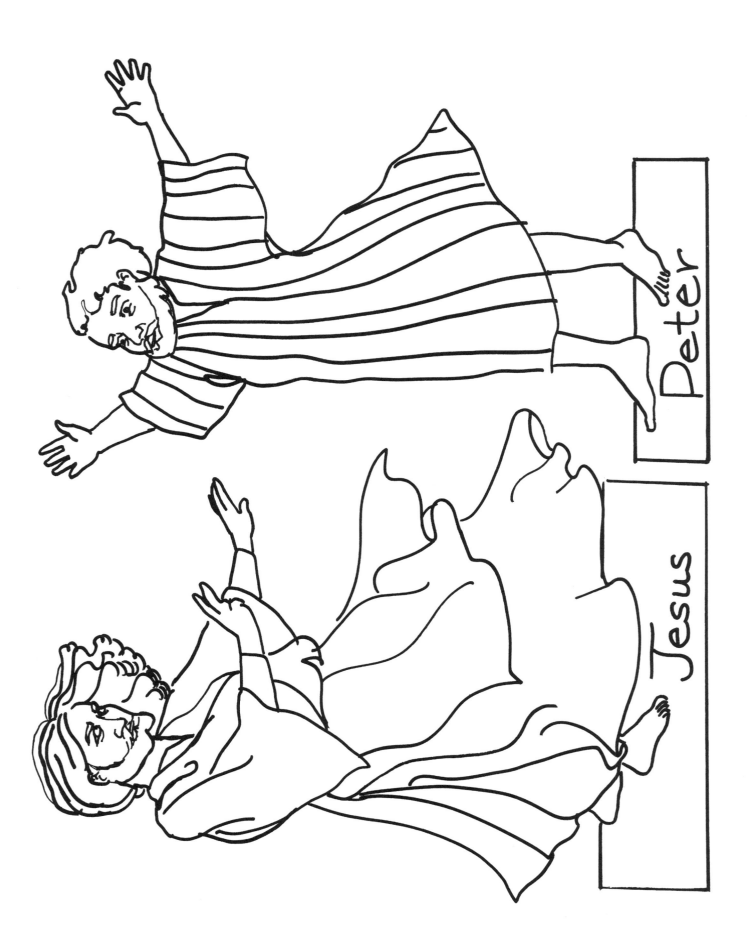

Peter

Jesus

# The Day the "Son" Shone

## A Story of the Transfiguration

Based on Matthew 17:1–9

### Questions to discuss before the story

Did you ever see someone who looked very happy? What did they look like?

### Preparation: Scene 1

*Puppets.* Peter, James, and John, Elijah, Moses, and Jesus.

*Prop.* A cloud.

*Backdrop.* A mountainside, a somewhat dark background as this Scripture story may have taken place at sunset or evening.

*Tips for this scene.* Copy the Jesus puppet twice. Color one in quiet, somber colors, such as browns and tans. Color the other as brightly as possible, in white and yellow, adding glitter or shiny star stickers to the puppet. Adhere both figures to one stick, one on either side so that Jesus is on both sides. The cloud should be colored so it too shines brightly, appearing rather mysterious. Adhere the stick to the top of the cloud so that it can be lowered from over the backdrop.

*Optional props.* A puppeteer can shine a flashlight up at the transfigured Jesus puppet, turning it on when the brightly colored puppet becomes visible, and turning it off as the "quiet colors side" faces the audience. A tube of face glitter can be used for an optional blessing ritual at the end of the play.

*The narrator stands to the side of the stage.*

| | |
|---|---|
| Narrator | One day Jesus took Peter, James, and John up a mountain. Jesus was going to die soon, so he wanted to give them a little glimpse of heaven. *Enter Jesus, "quiet colors side," and then Peter, James, and John. Have them start below the stage, gradually moving up, so it appears as if they are climbing. Jesus should end up in the center of the stage, while the apostles remain closer to one side.* |
| Narrator | Suddenly Jesus was transfigured, that is, he looked very different! *Turn Jesus around. A puppeteer can shine a flashlight on him.* |
| Narrator | His face shone like the sun! His clothing glistened and gleamed white as light! He was radiant, like an angel! The amazed apostles watched as two other figures appeared. *Enter Moses from one side, Elijah from the other. Both stand near Jesus on either side of him.* |
| Narrator | Peter, James, and John recognized them as holy men from ancient times. One was Moses, who had led his people out of Egypt. The other was Elijah, the great prophet! They stood near Jesus and talked with him. The apostles hardly knew what to say. Then Peter found his voice. "Lord," he said, "It is good to be here. If you wish, I will make three tents. I will make one for you, one for Moses, and one for Elijah." As he spoke, a bright cloud cast a shadow over them. *Enter the cloud from over the top of the backdrop.* |
| Narrator | Then God's voice came from the cloud. God said, "This is my beloved Son. I am well pleased with him. Listen to him." The frightened apostles looked around. Both Elijah *(exit Elijah to one side)* and Moses *(exit Moses to the other side)* were gone. So was the cloud. *Exit the cloud over the backdrop. Turn Jesus around, and turn off the flashlight.* |
| Narrator | Now there was only Jesus, Peter, James, and John. They began to walk down the mountain. *Exit puppets as if they were going down the mountain slowly. The narrator takes the tube of glitter* |

*and makes the sign of the cross on the children's foreheads with the glitter, telling them that they too are God's children.*

## For discussion and reflection
What do you think heaven will be like? What do we need to do to get to heaven?

## Closing prayer
*Leader:* Dear Jesus, long ago God said, "Let light shine out of darkness." And you, Jesus, have shone your light into our hearts. We believe and we say that you are Jesus the Lord!

*All:* Amen.

John

Jesus

James

Peter

Moses

Elijah

# Of Taxes and Trees

## A Story of Zacchaeus

### Questions to discuss before the story

Have you ever been unkind to someone who was different from you? How do you think that person felt?

### Preparation: Scene I

*Puppets.* Townspeople (which will need two sticks), Zacchaeus, and Jesus.

*Props.* The tree, with the space between the leaves and the trunk cut out so Zacchaeus can be seen through it. Anchor the tree to the stage by standing the stick in a ball of clay, then place it to one side of the stage.

*Backdrop.* The buildings for the city of Jericho on a tan poster board.

*Tips for this scene.* Zacchaeus could be a comic figure in the beginning. Children will identify with his smallness, and appreciate his humor. Then, too, his sincerity will be more pronounced when he speaks with Jesus.

*The narrator stands to the side of the stage.*

| | |
|---|---|
| Narrator | Jesus was coming to the city of Jericho! The townspeople were excited for they loved Jesus. *Enter the townspeople puppet on the side opposite the tree.* |
| Narrator | Soon a crowd lined up on the streets. They were waiting for Jesus to pass by. A man named Zacchaeus came along. *Enter Zacchaeus from the tree side.* |
| Narrator | Many people did not like or trust Zacchaeus. Zacchaeus collected their money for taxes. Sometimes, Zacchaeus cheated them. He took more money than he was supposed to. He kept the money for himself. Now Zacchaeus wanted to see Jesus, too. But he had a problem: he was a very short man. He tried and tried to get a better view, but he could not see over the crowd. *Zacchaeus "jumps" up and down behind the crowd, tries to see around, etc.* |
| Narrator | Then he had an idea! Zacchaeus ran further down the road and climbed a tree. *Zacchaeus climbs the tree.* |
| Narrator | He waited for Jesus to come down the road. *Jesus enters from the side near the crowd. He greets people but goes on walking.* |
| Narrator | When Jesus reached the tree, he called, "Zacchaeus! Come down quickly for today I must stay at your house." *Zacchaeus jumps down from the tree to stand by Jesus.* |
| Narrator | Zacchaeus was delighted! He jumped down and said, "Oh, thank you! I will be honored to have you visit." The other people grumbled. *Move the crowd back and forth a little.* |
| Narrator | "Why would Jesus stay with him?" they complained. "Zacchaeus has cheated us!" Zacchaeus said to Jesus, "I will give half of what I own to poor people. If I have cheated anyone, I will give them back four times as much!" Jesus smiled. "This is a good day. Our God in heaven rejoices because Zacchaeus has chosen to do what is right." *All the puppets exit. The tree is then removed.* |

### For discussion and reflection

How did people feel about Zacchaeus and why? Is it right to judge other people? Why not?

## Closing prayer

*Reader One:* Dear God, we all make mistakes and do wrong things, just like Zacchaeus.

*Reader Two:* Like him, we want to tell you we are sorry.

*Reader Three:* We will try to act in more loving ways toward others.

*Reader Four:* We know you love us. Thank you for forgiving us.

*All:* Amen.

# Jesus' Friends

## A Story of Martha, Mary, and Lazarus

Based on Luke 10:38–42, and John 11:1–46

**Questions to discuss before the story**

What makes a person a good friend?

**Preparation: Scene 1**

*Puppets.* Martha with water jar, Mary kneeling, and Jesus sitting.

*Prop.* A table. Attach two sticks to it, and secure these in clay so the table can stand freely on the stage and Martha can stand behind it.

*Backdrop.* The house of Mary, Martha, and Lazarus, on a neutral background. A typical house of the time had only one or two rooms. In these would be low stools, mats for sleeping, earthen jars for water and food, and an oil lamp. Foods that Martha may have been preparing for Jesus are bread, lentils, cucumbers, and wheat porridge.

*The narrator stands next to the stage. The table has been placed on the left of the stage.*

| | |
|---|---|
| Narrator | Jesus had many friends. Among his closest friends were two sisters named Mary and Martha and their brother Lazarus. They lived in a place called Bethany. Jesus visited them there. One day Martha began preparing dinner for Jesus and the family. *Enter Martha from below. She hurries about, going to the table and to other parts of the house.* |
| Narrator | When Jesus arrived, Martha welcomed him, and went on with her work. Mary, however, sat down and listened to Jesus. *Enter Jesus and Mary from below, in the center of the house. Martha stands behind the table.* |
| Narrator | Mary sat beside Jesus, at his feet. That's how a student used to sit to learn from a great teacher. But Martha was frustrated that Mary was not helping her. *Martha comes over to Jesus.* |
| Narrator | "Lord," Martha complained, "Don't you care that my sister is letting me do all the work? Tell her to help me!" Jesus looked at Martha. "Martha, Martha, you are anxious and worried about many things," he said. "But there is only one thing that is truly important. Mary has chosen that." *Exit all three puppets.* |

*When the backdrop for Scene 2 is put up, the table from Scene 1 is taken down.*

**Preparation: Scene 2**

*Puppets.* Martha with hands clasped, Mary standing, Jesus standing, a group of friends, and Lazarus.

*Props.* The stone for the tomb.

*Backdrop.* An outside scene with a cave-like tomb to one side. The opening into the cave is drawn on, but the stone is separate from the backdrop. The cave must be bigger than the stone. The opening into the cave must be smaller than the stone but larger than Lazarus. Make the cave look stone-like in color and texture, and the opening black, as if no light penetrates.

*Tips for this scene.* After coloring the opening to the cave black, cut along the outside edge of the opening on one side to form a slit. A puppeteer should hold the Lazarus puppet behind the backdrop, near the slit. When Jesus calls him forth, Lazarus slips through the slit and stands in the dark opening. The stone should be attached to the opening with one small piece of two-sided tape so a puppeteer can easily tug it and take it below. Also, when making the Lazarus puppet, explain to children that instead of using caskets, the Jewish people at that time carefully wrapped the body of a dead person in a clean, fine cloth called linen. Then they would place the body in a tomb. That's the reason for Lazarus' strange appearance.

*The narrator stands next to the stage.*

Narrator    Lazarus, the brother of Mary and Martha, became very sick and died. Jesus loved Mary, Martha, and Lazarus. So when he heard the news he traveled to Bethany. *Enter Jesus from the side farthest from the tomb.*

Narrator    Martha learned that Jesus had arrived and she hurried to him. *Enter Martha from the other side.*

Narrator    "Lord," she said. "If you had been here, my brother wouldn't have died. But still, I know that God will give you whatever you ask." Jesus said, "Your brother will rise." Martha agreed, "I know he will rise on the last day." Then Jesus said, "I am the Resurrection and the Life. Whoever believes in me, even if he dies, will live. Everyone who believes in me will never die. Do you believe this, Martha?" Martha nodded. "Yes, Lord, I believe that you are the Messiah, the Son of God." Then she said, "Now I must go tell Mary you are here. She is at home with friends." *Exit Martha to the same side she entered. Jesus remains. Enter Mary, Martha, and the group of friends. Mary runs to Jesus, the others remain a little behind her.*

Narrator    Like her sister, Mary said, "Lord, if you had been here, my brother wouldn't have died." And she began to cry. The friends were also crying. Jesus saw them weeping and he became deeply troubled. He asked, "Where have you laid him?" "Come and see," they said. *All the puppets walk toward the tomb.*

Narrator    Jesus, too, began to weep. Some of the friends said, "See how he loved Lazarus!" But some of the others said, "He cured others. Couldn't he have kept Lazarus from dying?" *They reach the tomb and stop.*

Narrator    The tomb was a cave. A huge stone was rolled in front of the opening. "Take away the stone," Jesus said. *The friends move close to the stone as if to move it. A puppeteer pulls the stone down from behind the puppets and takes it below.*

Narrator    Jesus looked up to heaven. He said, "Father, I thank you for hearing me. I know that you always hear me. But I say this so they will believe that you sent me." Then Jesus called out, "Lazarus, come out!" And Lazarus, who had been dead for four days, came out of the tomb! *Enter Lazarus through the door of the tomb. Mary and Martha rush to him.*

Narrator    Lazarus was wrapped in the burial wrappings. So Jesus said, "Help him so he can go free." *Exit all the puppets.*

Narrator    After this miracle, some were upset and wanted to kill Jesus. Others began to believe in him as Martha and Mary did.

## For discussion and reflection

How did Jesus show his friendship with Martha, Mary, and Lazarus—
   •in the first story?
   •in the second story?
How can you let Jesus be your friend?

## Closing prayer

Jesus, you help us and give us life. Like your friends Martha, Mary, and Lazarus, we say: We believe you are the Messiah, the Son of God.
*All:* Amen.

Group of Friends

Mary

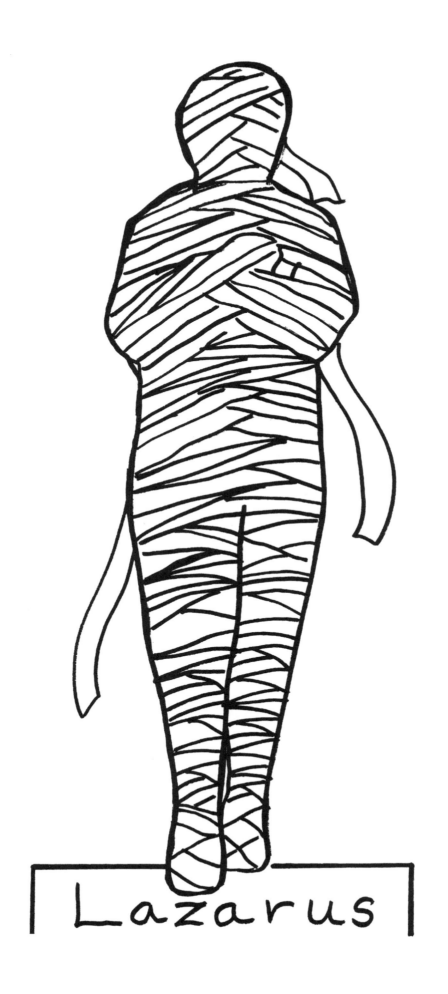

Lazarus

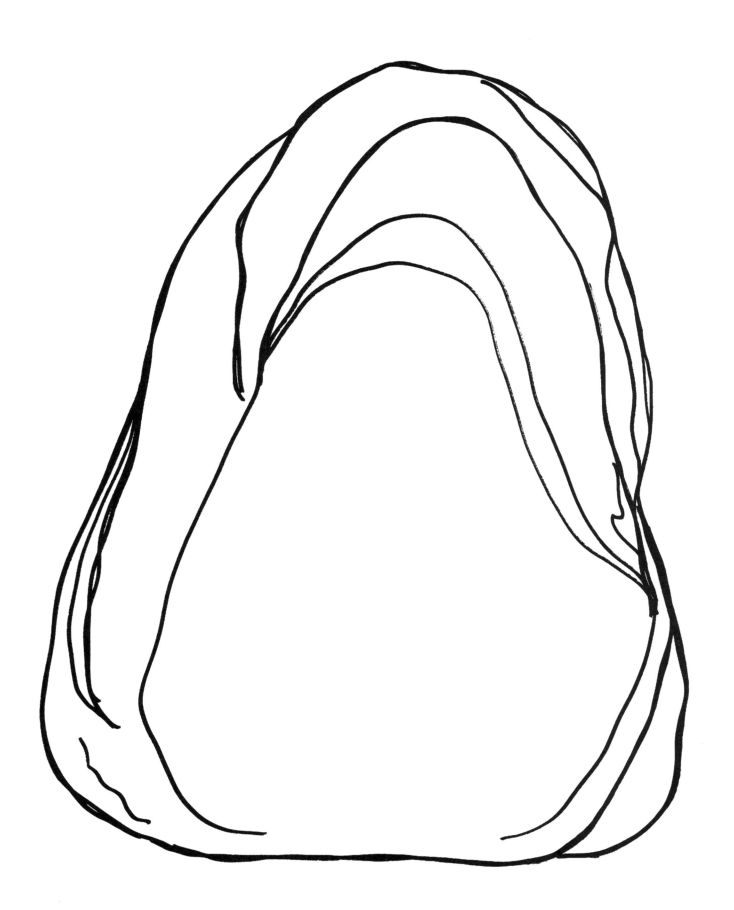

# Just As He Said

## A Story of the Resurrection

Based on Matthew 27:62–66; 28:1–10

### Questions to discuss before the story

Did you ever read or watch a rescue story where people who are in great danger are saved? How does everyone feel when the rescue is successful?

### Preparation: Scene 1

*Puppets.* Mary Magdalene, Mary the mother of James, the two soldiers, an angel, and Jesus.

*Props.* The stone for the tomb (found in Jesus' Friends story) and a cross or crucifix large enough for the audience to see.

*Backdrop.* The site of the tomb which was hewn out of rock. The sky should have the colors of dawn. According to John 19:41, this was in a garden. Place the tomb on one side of the backdrop.

*Tips for this scene.* As in the story of Lazarus, secure the stone to the tomb with a small piece of tape so a puppeteer can easily tug it down. The angel can be decorated with white glitter.

*The narrator stands next to the stage, holding up a cross or crucifix for all the audience to see, then brings the cross down and holds it reverently. (Later, when the audience's attention is focused on the stage, the narrator can discreetly place the cross behind the stage.) In a quiet manner, the narrator gives this explanation of what led up to this story.*

| | |
|---|---|
| Narrator | Jesus offered his life so that all our sins could be forgiven. The leaders in Jerusalem had heard Jesus say he would rise from the dead. They did not believe this. But after Jesus died on the cross, they were worried. They thought Jesus' friends might come and steal his body. Then his followers would say Jesus had risen. So the leaders sent soldiers to watch the tomb. *Enter the soldiers who go and stand on either side of the tomb.* |
| Narrator | Jesus' friends and disciples were frightened. Would they be killed, too? They were angry and very sad over Jesus' death. They were confused about why this had happened. The disciples did not know what to do next. There was only one thing they were sure of. They had to anoint Jesus' body with perfumes and spices. That's what family and friends did when a loved one died. *Enter Mary Magdalene and Mary from the side farthest from the tomb. They move slowly.* |
| Narrator | The morning sun touched the sky with a rosy light. Two women walked quietly down the road. Mary Magdalene and Mary, the mother of James, were on their way to Jesus' tomb. His body had been laid there after his death. Both women were wondering how they could move the huge stone away from the doorway of the tomb. They did not have to wonder long. As they came closer, they felt the ground begin to shake! *Shake the backdrop gently as well as all the puppets.* |
| Narrator | And as the earth shook, an angel of the Lord appeared! *Enter the angel from below.* |
| Narrator | He moved the stone away from the tomb. *The angel appears to move the stone as a puppeteer reaches up and pulls it off. The stone can be taken below.* |
| Narrator | The women and the soldiers stared at the angel. He was as bright as lightning. His clothing was as white as snow. The soldiers were so frightened, they fainted. They fell down as if they were dead. *The soldiers fall down and are taken below.* |
| Narrator | Then the angel spoke to the women. "Do not be afraid!" the angel said. "I know you have |

come looking for Jesus' body. Jesus is not here. He has risen from the dead, just as he said. Come, see where he was lying." *Mary Magdalene and Mary hurry over to the entrance to the cave and look in.*

Narrator     Mary Magdalene and Mary peered into the tomb. There was no body there! Then the angel said, "Go quickly. Tell the other disciples that Jesus has been raised from the dead. He will go to Galilee. They should go there and see Jesus. Now, I have told you." *Exit angel below. Mary Magdalene and Mary begin to walk away from the tomb.*

Narrator     Mary Magdalene and Mary were still frightened. But they were also overjoyed. Jesus was alive! He had come back to life, as he said he would! As they hurried off to tell Peter and the others, they saw someone standing on the path. *Enter Jesus.*

Narrator     He greeted them. The women cried out with joy. There in front of them was Jesus! *Mary Magdalene and Mary fall at Jesus' feet.*

Narrator     Joyfully they showed their love and respect for him. *Mary Magdalene and Mary stand up.*

Narrator     Jesus was happy to see them. He told them to tell the others that he was risen. *Exit all three puppets.*

Narrator     Jesus' friends taught many other people about his life, teachings, death, and resurrection. Those people taught others, who taught others. And now, centuries later, we still celebrate the miracle of Jesus' resurrection from death to new life. *The narrator leads the audience in singing "Alleluia!"*

## For discussion and reflection

How do you think Jesus' friends and followers felt after he died? And when they saw him alive again? Why is Jesus' resurrection so important for us?

## Closing prayer

Jesus is risen as he said. Alleluia! Alleluia!

*All:* Alleluia! Alleluia!

Soldier

Mary Mother of James

Mary Magdalene

Soldier     Angel     Jesus

# Bibliography

Baldwin, Rashim A. *You Are Your Child's First Teacher*. Berkeley, CA: Celestial Arts, 1989.

Lade, Roger, illustrated by Rob Shone. *The Most Excellent Book of How To Be a Puppeteer*. Brookfield, CT: Copper Beech Books, 1996.

Richmond, Arthur, Editor, illustrations by Remo Bufano. *Remo Bufano's Book of Puppetry*. New York: Macmillan Company, 1950.

Worrell, Estelle Ansley. *Be a Puppeteer! The Lively Puppet Book*. Orange, CA: McGraw-Hill Book Company, 1969.

# Of Related Interest...

## Stories of Saints through the Centuries
*Mystics & Martyrs, Healers & Hermits, Soldiers & Seekers...*
Anne E. Neuberger

Children will love these stories of heroic men and women who loved Jesus and lived by his example: Anthony of Egypt, Brigid of Ireland, Paul Miki, Martin de Porres, Edith Stein, just to name a few. Includes directions for helping the children make a timeline, as well as activities that connect the saints' examples to kids lives.     0-89622-984-X, 128 pp, $12.95 (J-31)

## Advent Stories and Activities
*Meeting Jesus through the Jesse Tree*
Anne E. Neuberger

Offers 24 ancient stories and symbols to mark the days before Christmas. Introduces children (7-12) to the tradition of keeping a Jesse Tree, with easy-to-follow directions for creating seven types of trees.     0-89622-734-0, 96 pp, $12.95 (B-22)

## Fun with Scripture
*Lectionary Word Searches and Bible Crossword Puzzles*
Jim & Audrey Alt and Patricia Kasten

This book contains reproducible crossword puzzles taken from the books of the Bible, and Lectionary word searches for the three cycles. A great way for teachers to help students learn more about Scripture while having fun at the same time.

1-58595-022-X, 112 pp, $12.95 (J-65)

## How Creative Catechists Use Stories
Janaan Manternach and Carl J. Pfeifer

This book uses popular children's literature to illustrate themes of compassion, community, forgiveness, and reconciliation. A wonderful, inspiring resource for teachers, catechists, parents, liturgists—anyone involved in handing on the faith to the young.     1-58595-112-9, 96 pp, $12.95 (J-73)

## Acting Out the Gospels
*40 Five-Minute Plays for Education and Worship*
Mary Kathleen Glavich, SND

Each of these ready-made gospel playlets can be incorporated into lessons on related topics or used to introduce/involve children in the Liturgy of the Word. They are adaptable to grades 4-8 and include stage directions, background notes, discussion questions, and a prayer activity.     0-89622-972-6, 128 pp, $14.95 (J-25)

## Acting Out the Miracles and Parables
*52 Five-Minute Plays for Education and Worship*
Mary Kathleen Glavich, SND

These 52 playlets, adaptable for all grades will enliven and enrich religion classes and "do learning" in a way that students will remember.     0-89622- 363-9, 144 pp, $12.95 (W-64)

*Available at religious bookstores or from:*

# TWENTY-THIRD PUBLICATIONS
PO BOX 180 · 185 WILLOW STREET   MYSTIC, CT 06355 · 1-800-321-0411
FAX: 1-800-572-0788   BAYARD   E-MAIL: ttpubs@aol.com
**Call for a free catalog**